WAKE UP...
LIVE THE LIFE YOU LOVE

FINDING LIFE'S
PASSION

WAKE UP... LIVE THE LIFE YOU LOVE
FINDING LIFE'S PASSION

Little Seed Publishing
Laguna Beach, CA

COPYRIGHT © 2006 by Global Partnership, LLC

Pre-Press Management by New Caledonian Press
Text Design: Justin Kimbro

Cover Design and Illustrations: K-Squared Designs, LLC

For information, contact Little Seed Publishing's operations office at Global Partnership: P.O. Box 894, Murray, KY 42071 or phone 270-753-5225 (CST).

Distributed by Global Partnership, LLC
608-B Main Street
Murray, KY 42071

Library of Congress Cataloguing In Publication Data
Wake Up... Live the Life You Love: Finding Life's Passion
ISBN: 1-933063-05-X

$14.95 USA $19.95 Canada

Other books by Steven E, and Lee Beard

Wake Up... Live the Life You Love

Wake Up... Live the Life You Love,
Second Edition

Wake Up... Shape Up... Live the Life You Love

Wake Up... Live the Life You Love,
Inspirational How-to Stories

Wake Up... Live the Life You Love,
In Beauty

Wake Up... Live the Life You Love,
Living on Purpose

Wake Up... Live the Life You Love,
Finding Your Life's Passion

Wake Up... Live the Life You Love,
Purpose, Passion, Abundance

Wake Up... Live the Life You Love,
Finding Personal Freedom

Wake Up... Live the Life You Love,
Seizing Your Success

Wake Up... Live the Life You Love,
Giving Gratitude

Wake Up... Live the Life You Love,
On the Enlightened Path

Wake Up... Live the Life You Love,
In Spirit

Wake Up... Live the Life You Love,
A Power Within

FINDING LIFE'S PASSION

How would you like to be in the next book with a fabulous group of best-selling authors? Another Wake Up book is coming soon!

Visit: WakeUpLive.com

We would like to provide you with a free gift to enhance this book experience. For your free gift, please visit: WakeUpGift.com

Table of Contents

Finding Life's Passion

Finding Life's Passion

FINDING LIFE'S PASSION

FOREWORD

Passion is pursuing hope through trials and failures; it is looking ahead to a light when the present seems so dark.

🖙 *Steven E*

In 2004, we published a book in this series titled *Finding Your Life's Passion*. We did so because so many of the successful people with whom we worked demonstrated in their lives the essential nature of passion. They told us how important it was to actually experience a deep-seated burning to achieve the goal; to believe so deeply in your purpose and your objective that a highly focused energy seems to want to burst forth, and your every waking moment is filled with a sense of awareness and drive. In dedicating the book, Steven E defined it in a way that speaks to the role of courage in passion, as you see, above.

We hope, in this book, that you may find the key to a life of passion. Not every door leads to the excitement of the purpose-centered existence. The path to passion for one may be, simply, an entertaining story. Perhaps it is a set of instructions that makes you believe that your passion may lie around the next turning of the page.

However, we firmly believe that the turning point for your life is almost certainly waiting in one of these chapters. Some have been brought back from the first bestselling version of this idea; others are new, and fresh, and filled with the promise that they can help you discover what a life's passion is and can do for you. We put this book in your hands, filled with the optimistic happiness that comes from knowing readers will see the vital nature of experiencing a passion for what they want most to do in life, and that this passion will drive them past all the barriers to success and fulfillment.

So, we join you, the reader, in thanking these contributing authors for the time it took to discover what they have to share, and to share it. We thank them for having the courage to put their names above their very private and, sometimes, painful thoughts and recollections so that you and I could take heart and hope. Most of all, we thank them for making possible the enormous creative power of passion in the hearts and minds of so many.

Our thanks, as well, to Bob Valentine and his staff at New Caledonian Press for their help in creating the book. Tami McQueen served as editorial coordinator, aided by editors Libby Lewis and Charissa Acree, and staff members Natalie Cunningham and Vicki Jo Stevens. Rita Oldham was the project manager, but she was interrupted for the happiest of reasons: the birth of her son Jayden Robert. Justin Kimbro, in designing the work, tried to create the same energy in typeface and image as our contributors address so eloquently.

Now, the hard work and the challenges are, literally, in your hands. Our hope is that one of these chapters will open the door to understanding and light the fire of passion that will power you to the realization of your dreams. Then, our passion will be rewarded, as well.

Lee Beard

MANIFESTING
Steven E

L et me explain how this works. We all have experienced a time when we thought of something and "bang" there it was. A thought in the mind and it becomes a material item. Everything you see was first a thought and then it became the chair that you are sitting on, or a pencil or a table. Everything is conceived before it becomes a physical object. Manifesting used to be this metaphysical concept that was not easy to explain. An example of this is seen when a quantum physicist is looking at the smallest particle. It appears, at first, in a hazy wave state. However, if he/she puts their concentration or observation on it, it will become a solid particle.

We live in a world where we see everything as being solid, but it is not solid at all. Even a rock, when it is broken down to its smallest particle, is in a hazy wave state. Now let me explain how you can put this into action. First, whatever we concentrate on will become more of our reality. If we want more health and a pain-free body, but we concentrate on how our back always hurts, we will get more pain. What we concentrate on will become greater. Keep your mind focused on your health, rather than lack of energy. Focus on the money that you do have, rather than that which you do not have.

Get a journal and begin writing about all the good you have. Each day write down things for which you are thankful. Concentrate on the things that you desire and watch them manifest into your life. Start learning about money; whose portrait is on the one, five, ten, twenty, fifty and hundred dollar bills. Treat money with respect as you would respect your health or family. Learn about the stock market and real estate. Buy books about people who have wealth. Get it out of your mind that money is bad, or it's evil. Money isn't evil. It's only a piece of paper!

You can be a loving, spiritual person, with plenty of money to share with your family and friends, or with worthy causes. Use your concentration and observation on money, happiness, health, love or whatever you desire, and watch the hazy wave particle turn into a solid form.

Steven E

Finding Life's Passion

Turn Your Passion into a Pay Day
Mick Moore

Have you ever noticed how certain goals that you set for yourself seem to manifest almost magically? Not one stumbling block, criticism or doubt seems to stop this kind of goal from becoming a reality. Then, there are other goals that seem to run out of steam before they even get off the ground. Have you ever wondered what causes some goals to skyrocket to success even though they may be more challenging than others? The answer is passion. Passion can be defined as the deepest desire to achieve a goal, no matter what the sacrifice.

Think of the dreams or plans you've set for yourself over the past ten or twenty years. Take a look at which goals or dreams became a reality and which ones fell short. If you look closely, you will see a trend in those that were successful and those that failed. It's probably pretty obvious which goals you were passionate about and which ones were not really important to you. Look at your career, the car you drive, the house you live in, your family or your spouse. Are you passionate about any of these things, or have you become the "living dead," dissatisfied with your career and personal life?

Consider my music career, for example. Some would say that I was fairly successful. I played with some of Rock's most popular bands. I recorded several albums that are still selling today, and I remain friends with the some of music's most famous celebrities. Yet could I have gone further? Could I have become more successful? The answer is a resounding, YES! Of course I could have, but the passion was no longer there. As soon as I started thinking about a new direction and new goals, my music career began to wind down. The music and shows didn't have that fire anymore. Instead, I set a new goal of becoming an internet entrepreneur. Creating multiple sources of income from the Internet became my main focus.

Goals are like seeds that you plant in the backyard. If you water them and nurture them, they grow. You don't have to dig them up everyday to see if the roots are spreading. You know such a seed is going to grow because you take care of it. If it gets cold outside, you bring it indoors. If it's dry, you water it. It is the same way with a goal you set for yourself. You tend to it every day. Metaphorically, you water it by taking action and doing whatever needs to be done to move that goal to the next level. You don't give up if you don't see immediate results. Just like the seed waiting to sprout, you know the magic is taking place. You are passionate about what you are doing and know that with persistence, your plan will bear fruit.

Many people have been lucky enough to find a new passion that has allowed them to make a substantial living working from home and working at their own pace, doing something they really feel passionate about. For many of us, the door to opportunity is the Internet. If your goals are to make more money and spend more quality time with family, I encourage you to look to the Internet. It provides a limitless assortment of career possibilities. There are sales-driven product sites, information and consulting sites, web design companies, and people buying and selling collectibles. The Internet continues to grow significantly in every major demographic area with nearly 80% of Americans using it. It's time to find your passion and turn it into a pay day! There's no time like the present to find a new passion for living and create new goals that will set your dreams and aspirations into motion. I did it, and I wrote the best-selling Home Business Success Kit to teach others how they can do it, too.

I want you to create a list, numbered 1-10, of ten things you enjoy doing more than anything else, such as golfing, fishing, or being funny. Now create a second list 1-10 of the things at which you are most talented. This may include cooking, bike riding, or telling jokes. Get together with family members or friends and have them start crossing things off both lists that they feel you're not that good at, until you have one "favorite" thing left and one "talent" thing left on each list. If you find that being funny is left on the favorite list, look back at how many of the goals or dreams you had that were somehow connected to your sense of humor. If you find that telling jokes was left on the talent list, look back at how many of the goals or dreams that you had that were somehow connected to your quick wit or your gift of gab.

The things you write on those two lists share the passion needed to achieve your goals and dreams. The more items you bring to play from both lists, the more motivated you will be to finish the goals you've set forth. Naturally, the opposite is true. If you didn't have any of the items from your two lists involved in a goal or dream, you probably gave up and quit on that goal long before you really got it started. With this in mind, take a long hard look at the current list of goals you're working on and see how many of them are really what you want to achieve and how many of them allow you to actually utilize your given traits and talents.

Finding Life's Passion

Do you have enough personal passion and drive behind your goals to ensure that you'll go the extra mile to successfully accomplish them? You may need to re-evaluate these goals to see whether they ignite the passion and spark that will keep you going through the exciting, challenging and possibly difficult days ahead. I encourage you to make several of these lists and share them with a partner, family or friends, so you can get an unbiased evaluation of your true gifts and talents. With this list in hand, there should be no doubt about where your passions truly lie. I feel so blessed not only to have found my passion—of helping others discover the entrepreneur in themselves—but also to have achieved many of the goals I've set for myself.

"Success is the result of dreaming more than is practical, doing more than is wise, risking more than is safe, and expecting more than is possible."

Mick Moore

Finding Life's Passion

Carpe Diem
Fernanda Alves Schmelz

What is your big dream? What do you feel passionate about? What was the secret of all those famous people who succeeded and left great legacies?

It's not what you do, your status, or money that make a difference. It is about believing in yourself enough to put your whole heart into doing what you love. It's about the focus of your passion. You can only become a winner as long as you do this and follow your purpose with passion.

You have to do what it takes to be a winner. Make a decision; define what your purpose and passion is. Don't let anyone stop or influence you. It's your life–your only life–take control of it. Otherwise, someone else will.

We all have passion and purpose. Have you found yours? If not, then you are not doing what you truly love. Many people study in a certain field because it runs in their family. For others, certain influences–perhaps certain people–made decisions for them. How do you expect to reach your ultimate goals this way? You need to focus on what you truly want, and then you will bloom like a beautiful flower.

The difference in people's success boils down to whether they have found their passionate purpose and if it is their focus. Your reality is the result of your focus, your attitude and your choices (thoughts, words and actions).

If you do what you love, you will feel an excitement and enthusiasm, and it will be a lot of fun. Are you one of those people who wishes that they were rather doing something else? What would it take for you to live a fulfilled and happy life?

Make your decision today; don't wait any longer. It's up to you. It exists deep inside all of us and wants to be set free.

We all have the drive to be successful, to fulfil our mission, to realize our dreams. It's like a burning desire, an inexplicable strength and force within each of us. Stop for a moment; make a decision to find your purpose. What is it, how are you going to get there, and when? Write it down; visualize it, and live as if it has come true. Sooner or later it will. Do it with desire, and you will live a life filled with passion. You will experience the greatest accomplishment by living the life you love.

Stop preparing for the future; rather, enjoy the present. We all seem to be preparing for retirement. What for? To look back and say what most people say, "I should have lived?" No matter how much we have, it never seems to be enough. It is not the quantity that counts; it's the quality of your life that truly matters.

Live your life–each moment–with magic. The poet challenges us, "Carpe diem." You will discover endless happiness within your true inner being. This way you will give and get the most out of life. Do what you love, and the rest will follow.

The purpose at this moment is to take action. Don't wait until tomorrow. We are all capable of contributing to a better world. It is essential for us to live our life to its full potential.

No matter who you are, what you do or where you come from, you are ready to begin. Have faith. Believe in yourself, focus and take the first step today! You do have a purpose in life. Take control of it and enjoy your journey.

Fernanda Alves Schmelz

INTERPERSONAL CREATIVITY: THE ART OF BRINGING THE BEST OUT OF OTHERS
Todd Creager

How does one live a life of passion? Life has taught me that I am most passionate when being creative. Having a passionate life involves actively designing my day, my week, and my year in a way that expresses who I am, my deepest values as well as my talents. We also have the ability to design relationships by treating others the way we want to be treated and by leading conversations and other forms of relating to higher ground.

Just as a musician can create a song and an artist can create a painting, we can develop interpersonal creativity. It is as important as any other kind of creativity, especially if we want to live our lives with passion. What do I mean by interpersonal creativity? Most of us go through life being interpersonally passive, reacting to those around us. If they do what we wish and make us feel comfortable, then everything is fine. However, the minute the other person does not fit our agenda, we react, either by trying to manipulate that person or by giving up or withdrawing.

The problem with this approach is that sooner or later (and probably sooner) someone will become a source of disappointment, anger or sadness to us and our natural energy and life enthusiasm will begin draining away. We cannot depend on others to fit our agenda in order to be happy, wealthy or fulfilled. The challenge for all of us is that our ancestors have not, on the whole, been great role models for interpersonal creativity. Reactivity has been the norm.

When I got married 22 years ago, I had no idea how ill-equipped I was to create a healthy marriage, one where both partners thrived and felt alive. Reactivity ruled. If my wife was pleased with me, my world was great; if she was angry or disappointed, I would usually return her anger or indignation. This would lead to more of the same patterns as one person would react to the other. Our life energy drained as did our enthusiasm for each other. There was a silver lining though. Through our trials and tribulations I learned that, as a marital partner, *I have influence*! Yes, I can actually convert a negative interaction into an opportunity to shift gears and bring out the best in my wife as well as myself.

Finding Life's Passion

Early in our marriage we had conflicts that got uglier and uglier as we continued to react. A therapist helped us chronicle the anatomy of an escalated conflict. Both of us felt justified in our reactivity and from our own point of view, we were absolutely correct. He helped us realize that we each had had many chances (at least a dozen each from beginning to full escalation of conflict) to make a different choice that would have changed the whole trajectory of the interaction. I had the power of positive influence but was wasting it on doing the immediate tension-reductive response, which ensured me of having more of exactly what I did not want from my wife. My marriage has now become a phenomenally useful arena in which I can learn how to be creative. Despite the fact that I sometimes forget to use my creative power, my "interpersonal creativity muscles" are growing. It is exciting and empowering to bring love, acceptance, and humility to a conflict that was laden with anger, judgment, and ego.

It makes common sense that the less energy we expend on maintaining conflict and keeping people limited, the more energy we have to fulfill our incredible potential in this lifetime. I have been a licensed marriage, family, and sex therapist for 22 years. I still get excited when I see partners who realize that it does not pay to be a victim. It is far more rewarding to take responsibility for maintaining negative interactions and then to choose, sometimes contrary to what our feelings are telling us, to do a constructive, uplifting behavior. I will always welcome those moments when a partner decides to stop protecting his or her own interests and truly listen to the other. No matter what pain the partner is feeling, I see softness and relief begin to return to the face. Everyone wins.

I am just as passionate when I counsel business leaders and managers in ways to evoke excellence in employees and co-workers. Leaders need to create an interpersonal environment that maximizes the probability that their employees will be inspired and motivated to do their best. Inwardly perceiving an employee as a failure, for example, is a surefire way to keep that employee limited. Leaders need to pay attention to how they perceive their staff and need to understand what a great effect their thinking as well as their words and behavior have on employee productivity. The workplace as well as marriage is a great arena in which to grow and to develop and bring more of one's highest self to the world.

I know that developing my own business has been a great character builder. I have run into many dead-end streets on the road to business success. The greatest thing

I have learned is to be passionate about other people's success and well-being. The more I am passionate about their good fortune, the less I have to worry about mine. I remember my early days of attending networking meetings. I was thinking only about how to get new clients. It was so similar to what I would do as a husband with the sole agenda of being perceived as "right." I was being egocentric and was receiving more of what I do not want from others. Ben Dean, head of MentorCoach, which is a group that trains therapists to do coaching, taught me a concept that he called "Servant Marketing." As I market myself, I am serving others. At networking meetings, I am now passionate about giving helpful information to everyone I meet, free of charge. What does that bring out of my fellow networkers? It brings out their trust, their gratitude, and in some cases their desire to hire me to assist them.

The amount of passion I have for life is directly proportional to the amount of time and energy I spend bringing the best out of others. As a husband, business consultant, therapist, speaker or author, it is clear to me that I am charged with that responsibility. In my CD, "Bringing the Best out of Others," I emphasize the importance of not being on automatic when it comes to our perceptions, words and behaviors. We all need to go against the gravitational pull of reactivity and find within our power to influence. The question I ask myself is, "How can I have maximum positive impact?" If I don't already know the answer I actually ask the person. It is all up to me, whether I live creatively or passively. Interpersonal creativity has been far more rewarding for me and I highly recommend it!

Todd Creager

FINDING LIFE'S PASSION

THE END IS IN THE JOURNEY
Tripp Mehew

It keeps me up at night. It makes my heart race, even without exercise. My eyes light up, my shoulders broaden, and my posture stands up to meet the sky. The feelings are nearly overwhelming–pride, satisfaction, happiness, eagerness, and a need to repeat it all over again. This is what passion is; and this is what keeps me alive.

I was almost angered by the fact that it took so long to find out what it was that drove me. I was in my late early 30's before stumbling on it. Sure, there were some signs but I had no idea that I would make this my life's work. How do you find it? Where does it come from? How long does it take to foster? And if I find it, then what?

You see, I wasn't a good kid. I tended to get into trouble. My parents were divorced and I think I was just acting out a little bit and taking advantage of the situation. It got so bad that I ended up in boot camp at MCRD San Diego on my twenty first birthday.

I joined the Marines! Wow, that was a wake-up call. The shock was felt all around my inner circle. My friends, family, and everyone I know couldn't believe it. "The Marines! Are you crazy? You will never survive." I heard that over and over again. What these people didn't realize is my drive, passion, and loyalty often made up for my erratic behavior. I think I just needed something to hang my hat on. Oh, and believe me, I had it. Suddenly I had structure, a solid job, a team, and a purpose.

I spent 6 years in the Marine Corps as a helicopter mechanic. I did a tour of duty in Persian Gulf. That is where I got my first taste of my passion. It occurred when our unit returned home. We landed in Bangor, Maine, upon our return from Saudi Arabia. What we returned to was surreal. I was met with hugs and cheers. People were crying and cheering for us. I wore that uniform proudly that day. In truth, I just wanted to go get a good ol' Budweiser from the bar. But I also got a taste of something that really drove me.

My second meeting with my passion came with the birth of my son, Sebastian. In an instant my focus and dedication turned. Life was no longer about me. Life was about helping this little baby turn into a man. I was a natural at fatherhood. It just seemed so easy to care. There are so many trials and tribulations in growing up. A child needs someone to give guidance and to teach strong morals; he needs someone to listen. This experience drove me even closer to my passion.

I finished my 6 years along with my schooling at Embry Riddle Aeronautical University and went to work, where I climbed the ranks of the corporate ladder. I did well and was paid well for my work. But in truth, what I really enjoyed was helping 5-, 6-, and 7-year-old kids understand and enjoy the game of baseball. I was a little league coach and I loved it. A base-clearing triple by one of my kids was the best feeling in the world. I coached for 7 years.

In my late 20's, I took a job at a start-up telecom company in San Diego as a mechanical engineer. Once again I was paid well for my services, but I wasn't happy. The corporate world, the commute, and my job were just not satisfying. Then came the tragedy of 9/11. My company folded and jobs were scarce. I bought a pool route to pay the mortgage.

Although cleaning pools wasn't the best job in the world, it gave me time to coach little league, spend more time with my family, and start a second business from home in network marketing. I had time to ponder my existence, my needs, my wants, and my future. Brushing pool walls definitely gives you time to think about other things.

I came up with an idea to help Veterans who were transitioning from military to civilian life. I wanted to convince them that the skills they learned in the military more than prepared them to seek their own destiny. They didn't have to punch a time clock or work for someone else if they didn't want to. Many of them were very excited at the thought of owning their own business. Because of my own experiences and my desire and ability to encourage and motivate, I was able to help many Vets. I would beam with pride when they succeeded.

Suddenly it came to me. It's what I'm good at. It's what drives me. I found my passion–helping other people achieve goals that they thought were unachievable. Sebastian never thought he could hit a gaming-winning triple in the last inning. One of my Vet friends never even thought of owning his own real estate company.

Now he makes a six-figure income. Those Americans in Maine felt that we saved them somehow. We were heroes. We helped them. But I got more pleasure watching them enjoy the success that they obviously felt.

My passion is helping others realize that they have what it takes. Finding your passion is not a treasure hunt for gold at the end of a rainbow. Some find it early in life; some take 50 years to find it. What is important is that you continually search until it is yours. It's that thing that makes you stand taller, smile wider, and tingle inside. You will know it when you feel it. Start your journey and find your passion.

Tripp Mehew

Finding Life's Passion

"Cause" it to Happen!
Gregory Scott Reid

There is a universal truth that states, "People will do more for a 'cause' than they would ever do for money." Don't believe me? Let me ask you, would you let me shoot you in the chest with a handgun for $10,000? Probably not, right? Now, what if someone came into a local restaurant and pointed that same gun at your child, spouse or parent–would consider throwing yourself in the line of fire to save their life? Perhaps.

What's the difference? There was a 'cause'–an underlining purpose for your rational. This same cause is, in effect, what controls the world through its wars, religion, and political beliefs. The same way a pilot would crash his plane into a ship in combat, strap an exploding vest to his chest, or again, take a bullet for someone they love.

Here is where you may say to yourself, "Ok, I get that, but what does that have to do with me?" Answer... Everything!

Another term of this cause may be described as "passion." Something that you are so committed to that you would sacrifice, risk, and offer all you have to see it through to the end. Once we find this passion, it will grip us, consume us and carry us through any obstacles or barriers we may face.

Let's switch gears here for a second. You have heard all the statistics about new businesses that fail. Want to know the overwhelming reason why? It's not due to the lack of investment capital, market share, or even the type of business in question. It's because they have not made this shift from passion. In other words, they have not made this new venture their "cause," but more from their interest.

Let me explain. Fact is, most people opening a new business or choosing a career move toward something they are 'interested' in, rather than something in which they are committed.

Imagine a personal relationship, one where you were simply interested in the other person. They may be attractive at the moment, but again, you are only interested in them. As soon as obstacles arise, which they will, what will happen? You're out the door, right? Imagine the same relationship, where you are now 'committed' to it, one where you married the person, and decided through thick and thin you will dedicate your life to make it work. When the same obstacles come your way, chances are, you will work through them rather than take off running.

The same analogy applies toward business and anything else in life. Once we find this passion, our cause, it becomes the fire that keeps the engines burning. Fear no longer becomes a factor. Our passion ignites the sparks to our soul and will become the beacon of light through all the dark times.

Have you ever met someone who was on their life's mission? They were dedicated to becoming a champion in sport, perhaps they want to create an orphanage for the underprivileged, or save the whales? You see it in their eyes, don't you? That look of commitment to their cause, this internal passion we speak of. They never let obstacles stand in their way; while maintaining the best of attitudes, and happy disposition. They always seek opportunity to gain just one step closer toward their goal.

Want some good news? You can have this fire too. The secret is to discover our cause, our mission, our passion and then pursue it with everything we have.

It's been said, "Life is a professional sport, don't play it as an amateur." Let me ask you something? The same question you heard from someone years ago, but never really focused on... what would you do with your life if you knew for certain you could not fail? What would that be? What would your life look like? Would you become a teacher? Write a book? Star in a movie? What? When you were a kid, and someone asked you what you wanted to be when you grew up, is that what you are doing today?

Here's the moral. Life is short, and our dreams are long, long overdue. So I offer you this challenge. State it and create it! Set some free time aside for yourself and ask—"What would I do if I had all the money in the world?" State it aloud!

Would you continue to work in that cubicle and fear placing your lunch in the fridge because someone might take it? Would you keep putting up with a boss who treated you less than kind? If the answer is no, then it's time to realize this simple truth–we are exactly where we choose to be and it's time to move toward a brighter path.

Once we decide we want more, and are willing to go to any lengths to get it, this is where the miracle begins. This is the turning point when our focus goes from needs to wants. The time we ask ourselves, what is our cause? What is our mission, purpose, and ultimate plan for our time on this spinning rock?

Today is the day to begin living the same way as the dreamers we spoke about earlier. The ones who would do anything for their dream.

It's up to you–now go find yours and then 'cause' it to happen! Best wishes and keep smilin'.

Gregory Scott Reid

FINDING LIFE'S PASSION

Finding Life's Passion

The Look That Changed My Life!
Earl D. Darling

I was born in Kingston, Jamaica, to very poor parents who struggled to put food on the table. My mother was ambitious and dreamed of going to America and bringing the family there. When I was 14 years old, my mother fulfilled her dream. She was sponsored by a very kind lady who took her to America to work for her. Mom worked hard, and in the course of several years, she brought most of the family to America.

I came to America with my brother, Nick, in 1969, just a few months before my 21st birthday. I remembered that plane ride very well, as it was the first time I had ever flown. It was dark as the plane began its descent to Kennedy airport, and as I looked over the sea of lights, I was awed by the beauty and bursting with excitement.

America: I had heard so much about her. I was told the streets were paved with gold and money grew on trees. I heard people even gave money away through a strange custom called "tipping," with which I was not familiar. My plan was to work as a hotel bellboy and be the recipient of those generous tips. America had been described to me as the land of opportunity, where even a high-school dropout like me could get a job and make more money than most of the educated folks back in Jamaica. I could not wait to pick up some easy money and walk on golden streets. But reality set in on me quickly. I discovered there were no money trees, no golden streets, and no bellboy jobs available where I was living. Here I was, in America, the Promised Land, but I could not cash in on the opportunities because I had very little education, no job experience, no car, and no credit.

Eventually I found a job at a local supermarket stocking shelves and gathering shopping carts from the parking lot. I earned about $80.00 per week, which was good money to me. I had arrived! I was content and comfortable, until one day something happened to upset the whole applecart. One morning I got up with my usual cheerfulness, walked to work, and began stocking shelves. As I looked down the aisle I saw a lady walking toward me. It turned out I knew this lady . . . she was my mother!

Mother walked right up to me and I was about to greet her, but on her face was the sternest look I had ever seen on man or animal. She looked at me with such intensity I could feel her eyes penetrating my soul. She didn't say a word but her eyes spoke volumes. This was what I heard, "My son, I came to this country and worked like a slave so you could make something of your life. But look at you; you have no ambition or desire. You are content stocking shelves for the rest of your life. Is this it? Is this all you want? What a waste! I expected great things of you and I'm very disappointed. What are you going to do with your life?"

Mother's stare may have lasted only a few seconds but it felt like an eternity. I was disarmed and defenseless, and I went home that night a beaten young man. She had just given me the worst beating I'd ever had–not with a belt, but with her eyes. There was nothing wrong with me working in a supermarket, except that I was about to make a career out of stocking shelves. Mom knew I had the ability to do a lot more with my life!

That night I was very troubled in my spirit. I knew I had to do something, but I didn't know what to do. I loved my mom, and the look of disappointment on her face was breaking my heart. Suddenly I had the strangest idea to do something I had never done before. I got a sheet of paper, found a pen, and began to design the life I really wanted. Some of my desires were a high school equivalency diploma, driver's license, car, high-paying professional job, wife, income-producing house, and college degree. After I completed my list, I immediately took action and began working toward the goals I'd written. There was never a doubt in my mind that I would accomplish everything.

I enrolled in night classes in an adult education program and got my GED. My mom taught me how to drive in America. I had learned to drive in Jamaica but found out Americans drive on the "wrong" side of the road. I was scared and intimidated by the big highways and the volume of traffic and how fast everyone drove, but I soon mastered the beast and got my driver's license. I saved enough money from my supermarket job to buy my first car.

One day I received a piece of mail promoting a 6-month course in COBOL from the Institute of Computer Technology. How in the world I got on their mailing list so quickly I do not know. I wanted a professional job, and a computer programmer was indeed a high-paying professional job. I was able to borrow the money and complete the course. Within a few years I was working as a computer programmer for a major pharmaceutical company. I met a wonderful woman, got

FINDING LIFE'S PASSION

married, had a family, and bought our first income-producing three-family home. It wasn't long before I completed my BA degree, Summa Cum Laude.

That one look from my mother helped me discover the incredible power of goal-setting to give direction to my life. Goal-setting became a life-long practice for me. With belief in goal attainment, backed by persistent action, I have continued to live my dream. I bought and sold other income-producing properties and eventually bought my dream house. I continued my education and earned an Executive MBA degree. Goals helped me overcome the loss of loved ones, financial reversals, and self-destructive habits. They've helped me chart a new course in a life filled with faith, hope and positive expectation, even after experiencing the death of my wife from cancer and the loss of my daughter in the World Trade Center terrorist attack on September 11, 2001.

By the divine hand of God, the help of a wonderful mother, and the support of my first wife, Margaret, and current wife, Gwen, I discovered the goal-setting strategies that released the potential within me. I also discovered that success is not an accident and that there are specific things you must learn and apply in order to wake up the giant within. I have found my passion in life and that is to help others unlock their God-given potential and live life to the fullest. My passion today is to develop a world-wide ministry dedicated to helping others grow and achieve total freedom and optimum health in spirit, soul, and body.

Earl D Darling

A PASSION FOR WISDOM
Alan Hewitt

"Passion" and "emotion" are often confused. Unbridled emotion can easily take us off the track; passion for truth, life, and those we love will keep us focussed on that which is most important. Consider three acts of passion which kept emotion in check.

Can You Reap Before You Sow?

Parenthood is a great laboratory for personal growth—for both parents and children. My son, Jack, is 10-years-old. We have an arrangement that if he hasn't done his homework before Sunday, he can't play computer games or watch TV (which he doesn't get to do during the school week) until he finishes it. As usual, on the way home from his soccer match on Sunday morning, he tried to negotiate a way to play a game first and do his homework later. This made me think of something and I was surprised at how well it worked.

Jim Rohn often uses biblical references for much of his wisdom and the one that I used with Jack was about sowing and reaping. I said, "Pretend you're a farmer who plants crops and your job is to tend the crop, pull out weeds, water it, fertilize it and then when it's ready, you get to harvest the crop."

Jack said, "Yep, OK."

I asked, "Well, what do you think would happen if you didn't plant the crop or look after it? Do you think you'd get to harvest?"

Jack said, "No."

Then I asked, "What if you yelled at the ground and said 'Give me a crop!' Do you think that would help?"

Jack laughed and agreed that it wouldn't. I told him that this was like his wanting to play the game before he did his homework. Instead, he needs to plant a crop first, that is, do his homework and then he can have his harvest (reward), because that's the way things work best. Jack really got the concept and did his homework cheerfully and got his "harvest" in due course.

Why am I telling you this? It seems to me that this concept is something that we all tend to forget at times–the people who reap great rewards in life are those who have planted lots of crops (have taken action), tended those crops, and had the patience to wait until the harvest.

Are You Thinking Accurately?

Last night, just a minute or so after I got home with Lesley and the kids after being out for the evening, we heard a loud bang. I was coming out of the garage and I thought something had fallen in there. Since it was late, I decided to wait until morning to check it out. The next morning I'd forgotten about it. When I went out the front door I saw a red house brick in front of the door. The left-hand glass side panel had red dust and a slight scratch! Someone had obviously thrown this brick from just a few feet away. Luckily; it had bounced off. That explained the noise we heard the night before. I called and made a police report.

The incident made me think about the motive of the person throwing the brick and my own reaction to it. You see, I could have allowed myself all sorts of unhelpful thoughts, such as, "Someone's out to get me," or "The neighbourhood we live in is dangerous." I could have started living in fear. Someone once said, "A life full of fear is a life half lived." I chose to conclude that it was a random act of violence that would probably never happen again. "Thinking accurately" means putting things into proper perspective and not jumping to conclusions. It can be make life a lot less stressful.

When Does Peppermint Tea = Ginger Tea?

A couple of weeks ago, I was having lunch with my wife, Lesley, in a cafe in the Swan Valley here in Perth, Australia. There were a number of teas available by the pot; we decided to order "Refreshing Ginger." A few minutes later our tea arrived and we poured ourselves a cup each. After it had cooled a bit, I took a sip and realized straight away that it was peppermint, not ginger. I called a waitress over and asked for the ginger tea instead.

FINDING LIFE'S PASSION

What happened next has an interesting lesson about "reality." A couple of minutes later, the waitress came over with the young lady from the kitchen who had prepared the tea. She had in her hands a tea canister with "Ginger Tea" written on it. She went on to explain that she had made the tea with the correct leaves. I asked her to open the lid, and immediately Lesley and I smelled peppermint. I told her that it smelled like peppermint, but she pointed again to the canister (a generic type refilled over and over again) with the "Ginger Tea" label. Because of the label, she was convinced that it was ginger–regardless of smell or taste! We realized that we weren't going to get ginger tea that day, so we had a laugh and told her we'd have the ginger tea that smells and tastes like peppermint.

This incident is a great illustration of preconceived ideas. I suppose that everyone has them at times. We often don't see things as they are, but as WE are, according to the labels we've put on them–our map of reality. Fortunately, meditation can help us bring our map of reality and reality itself closer together over time. We start seeing things as they actually are. Perception and reality – it's important to be able to distinguish the two!

Alan Hewitt

FINDING LIFE'S PASSION

YOU NEVER KNOW AND THE REST IS HISTORY!
Lou & Carla Ferrigno

I was taking a break from being in therapy, and I was managing a restaurant when I was called to the front door one night. A very large man was standing there taking up the entire doorway. He was really taken a back because I was a woman and the manager. He asked if his party could be seated even though some of the guys were under age. Because we had an open bar, I told him that was not possible. Even though he asked several times I would not allow them to be seated. My staff swarmed around me when he left, and said, "How could you do that?" They could not believe that I had thrown out "The Incredible Hulk." I had never seen his show, which was enjoying considerable popularity in those days.

The following Friday evening, he returned with his stunt double. Now I didn't remember who he was from the time before but as I passed by his table, he asked if I would sit down and talk with him. Since I was the only woman manager with the chain at the time, I made it a policy to never sit down and visit with the restaurant patrons. As I came by the table again, he asked if I would sit down with them and again I said, "No." However, he kept asking and his eyes were just so sweet, I finally sat down for a few minutes. I never dated men that were big, Italian or Scorpios.

He asked if he could take me to breakfast and, again, I declined. He told me he had to attend a party and that Dolly Parton would be there. He wanted me to go with him. I told him, "No." He asked for my phone number and I told him, "No." Again, after he persisted, I took his number and I told him I might call him. You guessed it! I called and, as they say, the rest is history.

The next day after the party, I told my mother that I had met the man that I was going to marry. We were never apart from that time on.

At our first meeting, Lou knew something I had yet to learn. Despite the many rejections I threw in his path, his passion to include me in his life carried him forward. Of course, I am grateful that it did.

His passion came from his experience in achieving fame as he overcame fear and human frailty. He became an international figure because of his drive–his unstoppable drive–to accomplish his goals.

Now, 24 years and three wonderful children later, I love the entertainment and training business that is part of my life. However, my greatest joy is my life with Lou and our family. That joy is a gift of his passion, and your passion, once found, will bring you joy, too.

Carla Ferrigno

Finding Life's Passion

On-going Journey
Anita Narayan

Living the life I love started when I learned one very fundamental thing–transformation happens when you unlock your potential and develop inner resources.

In March 2000, my career involved very long hours, and I was feeling restricted and unfulfilled. I noticed other things that were extremely important to me were neglected. The lifestyle of freedom I was seeking would not be fulfilled had I remained in my work environment. I was afraid of failure and lacked self-confidence when it came to starting a business–something about the security of a pay check. There was not an external event that could give me the confidence I needed. These were issues left to inner resources. My mindset and outlook began to change when I attended a Tony Robbins event at Wembley called "Unleash the Power Within."

It was this event that began my journey to accessing tools to strengthen my inner resources and unlock my potential. I learned how to motivate myself toward change.

My first change was to invest in my own personal development. I attended a university life mastery course. Like driving a car, the real learning came after I got the piece of paper. I continued to expose myself to the things I had already learned so the lessons would take root and recondition my thinking. After all, old habits die hard. I learned and practiced accelerated techniques to aid my absorption and assimilate new knowledge.

I have a passion for football, personal development, and health. Since March 2000, I have gone on to start my own life coaching business, and I now specialize in accelerated learning techniques and peak performance coaching. Through my life coaching practice, I take joy in seeing the lives of others transformed personally and professionally. By applying principles of peak performance, I extended my career in women's league football and at 40-years-old, I was picked again to play for the region. I have earned a certificate in football coaching.

Finding Life's Passion

Living the life I love is not a destination but an on-going journey. There are some key lessons I have learned along the way which have proved instrumental in the lifestyle I am now cultivating, and which I continue to learn and translate. I have learned to ask different questions of my life. I now ask "How Can I?" instead of "Can I?" The brain responds to questions just like a computer responds to a search for a keyword and will seek to answer that question.

I have also learned that environment is important to growth. I have surrounded myself with quality friends who share and cultivate similar core values such as honesty, fun, empathy, a positive outlook, contribution to others, compassion, and growth. A tool that has had great impact on my growth has been the Center Pointe Program, which uses sound technology through passive listening to induce states of deep rest and relaxation, while helping my brain evolve to higher levels of functioning. This has enabled me to acknowledge and release emotions rather than suppress them. I have acquired deeper states of calm and composure during challenging times.

Having a personal coach has given me the synergy and focus to aid my endeavours. I have also learned to see failure and mistakes as an important part of the fabric of success rather than its antithesis. I compare life to football. It is a contact sport where there is a clear goal of winning the match but also an acceptance that I will get tackled at some stage. I have discovered that when I let go of what I cannot control, I access a more resourceful state where creative energy helps me find resolution, solutions and new possibilities.

I have shared with you joys and challenges in the hope that you can see that living the life you love is not about smooth sailing. It is exciting nevertheless. What ultimately determines our experience in life depends on our inner resources and commitment to growth. Growth brings its new opportunities along with a fruitful and exciting life. There is no other place I would rather be!

Anita Narayan

FINDING YOUR PURPOSE
Fabienne Fredrickson

People often ask me how I came to find my life's purpose as a successful business coach to thousands of entrepreneurs, a published author, and speaker on the topic of Client Attraction. It all comes down to one defining moment in late 1999. That defining moment led me to teaching entrepreneurs how to easily and consistently get new clients. I'd recently quit my corporate job in advertising and taken a great leap of faith to start a private nutrition practice out of my tiny 300-square-foot apartment in New York City. I'd gotten clients right away, but not enough to pay my big-city rent and my bills each month.

The credit card companies were calling daily, wanting their payments. Every time I heard those messages, my stomach would turn into knots. I stopped answering the phone and started tossing and turning at night with what I now call the "3:00 a.m. I-don't-have-enough-clients sweats." I had officially hit rock bottom.

Desperate, I called my dad in the middle of the night. With tears rolling down my face, I told him about my practice. Yes, my clients were very happy with my work, but I didn't have enough clients to stay afloat for 3 months. He sat quietly listening to me and then said, "Fabienne, if there's anything I know about you, anything at all, it's that when you want something, and you want it badly enough, there's nothing that's going to stop you from getting it. So, figure out how you're going to get clients, and then go and do it."

For some, that may sound like a "duh" moment. For me, it came down to "Figure it out or throw in the towel." Because I wasn't willing to go back to the corporate world, I made a commitment to learn absolutely everything that had to do with getting clients. I read every book on marketing and networking. I paid for courses with my non-maxed-out credit cards; I borrowed books, went to seminars—you name it. It was exhausting.

Here's what I learned: there was no one teaching the entire marketing process for attracting clients, packaging your services, closing the sale virtually every time (without feeling sleazy), and creating systems so this would happen again and again, without fail. Nowhere was this information available in one place. I wanted to create a process for myself that I could replicate endlessly so I would never have to experience the famine again. I made it my task to create the "Client Attraction System." Each step would be verifiable and repeatable.

I sometimes made costly marketing mistakes. More than once, I cried from sheer frustration. But I kept going, because there was no other alternative. It paid off. Within less than 8 months, I was at full capacity: 31 clients! During this process, I had a life-changing epiphany.

As soon as I learned how to attract clients easily, marketing actually became fun for me. What I enjoyed most about being an entrepreneur became marketing, not teaching clients how to cook brown rice or steam tofu. I knew how to make authentic marketing work.

Soon, other entrepreneurs started asking for my help. I'd give them a couple of things to do. Virtually every time, the person called me later saying, "It worked! I got a new client!" This happened with dozens of people. It was wonderful to see others succeed using my "Client Attraction System." Because I got so much pleasure doing something for others (for free), I knew that I had found my purpose.

Entrepreneurs kept calling. It seemed like a sign from the Universe, a loud knock on the door of opportunity. I soon stopped doing nutrition and moved into a coaching practice. I began teaching entrepreneurs to get more clients, enjoy self-employment and have more money and more fun. Since I began coaching, I've worked with thousands of private clients and groups and have spoken to audiences of 1,200 people. I have published the "Client Attraction Home Study System," a how-to series of 10 important business-building steps that entrepreneurs can follow in order to get more clients, in record time.

I now bring in six-figure yearly revenues and work only 9 to 12 days a month with 14 weeks of vacation per year. I've cleared all my credit card debt (for good), we live in a great house at the beach, and I'm on my way to seven-figure revenues within the next few years. Don't get me wrong. It's great to have money and nice things, but it's the freedom and ease of living my purpose that is the most rewarding. Work isn't a hardship or struggle anymore, and I'm home at 5:15 p.m. every day to be with my husband and play with my children. I know that these same benefits are available to anyone.

Here's what I learned about finding my purpose:

1. When you're not aligned with your purpose, life is more of a struggle.
2. Hardship is actually good. It's a sign from the Universe that you're not necessarily on the right track. See hardship as a blessing; it's a clue that you need to change your direction.
3. Look around for signs. They're everywhere if you look for them. Little happy coincidences aren't coincidences at all. They're signs. If you act upon them and take inspired action, you'll expedite your journey to living your purpose.
4. Find what comes easily to you, what helps others and makes you feel good at the same time. If something brings you joy (like, for me, teaching and inspiring entrepreneurs to truly succeed) then it's something to pursue.

Here are questions to ask yourself to help you find your own purpose:

1. What section of the bookstore do you gravitate toward? Take a look at your bookshelf and nightstand. What topic do you love most? That's an indication of what your purpose is. I was reading success-mindset and marketing books on my honeymoon and it didn't feel like work.
2. What is the greatest challenge you have overcome? Your purpose might be helping others overcome similar challenges.
3. What's your before-and-after story?
4. Look for the path of least resistance: what brings the most meaning to your life?
5. If money weren't an issue and you had all the money you needed, what would you do for free to make a difference in the world?

Your purpose is to help others and to feel good doing it. Once you find it, throw yourself into it. Remember, though, sometimes our resolve gets tested to show how badly we want something. Don't give up. Do what it takes to make it happen, no matter what setbacks occur. Success will naturally come to you when you do. You won't believe you are getting paid to live a life of purpose.

Fabienne Fredrickson

PASSIONATE CONSCIOUSNESS
Bill Harris

Up until about age 40, I was definitely not living the life I loved. I was chronically angry, often depressed, and had one abysmal relationship after another, most ending in intense heartache. I had no real career and no idea how to create one. The direction of my life was down—at best, sideways.

This was all a blessing in disguise, though, because it created an intense motivation to learn what happy, peaceful, and successful people were doing that I wasn't.

Today, I'm married to a wonderful woman who really loves me. I make ten times what I used to fantasize about in my wildest financial dreams. And, I have a challenging career doing something I love.

What's more, my anger problem is gone—and I haven't been depressed for even one minute in nearly fifteen years.

Now, at age 54, I truly am living the life I love.

This transformation happened because I discovered a few key principles that created tremendous positive change for me. They will work for you, too.

What are these secrets?

First, happy people acknowledge that they are creating their reality, internally and externally. They see circumstances as an influence, but know that what they do inside creates how they feel and behave, and what people and situations they draw to themselves.

For most people, this processing of external circumstances happens unconsciously—out of awareness. This makes it seem as if circumstances cause your feelings and behavior and what you attract into your life. When this happens, it seems as if you are at the effect of external causes over which you have no control. You feel like a puppet. When things are good, you feel good. When they're bad, you feel bad. Happy people, however, even if they can't see how they're creating what is happening, know that they are. They take responsibility.

Another characteristic of happy people is that they act because of the possibilities they see. Where the unhappy person sees a challenge as impossible, the happy person sees what is possible. And, by focusing on what is possible, happy people make those possibilities come true.

A third characteristic of happy, successful people: they focus their mind on what they want and keep their mind off of what they do not want.

Here's what I mean by focus. When you think, you make what psychologists call internal representations: pictures, sounds, feelings, smells, tastes, or internal dialog. When you focus on something, you create an internal representation of it using one of these six thinking modalities.

These internal representations can be of what you want... or of what you don't want. Take prosperity, for instance. You could focus on not being poor, or you could focus on being rich. That is, you could make a picture inside of poverty, wanting to move away from it, or you could create a picture of being wealthy, wanting to move toward it.

In both cases the intention is the same, but your brain doesn't care about your intention. It just sees the literal content of the picture. When you focus on riches, it thinks you want riches, and motivates you to see opportunities, find resources, and take action to be rich. When you focus on not being poor, it sees a picture of being poor, and motivates you to see opportunities, find resources, and take action... to be poor.

Most people focus on what they want to avoid without realizing the consequences of doing so. When they get what they focused on, they assume they didn't focus hard enough and redouble their efforts. This creates even more of what they don't want, which creates more frustration.

The other penalty for focusing on what you don't want is that you feel bad. In fact, all bad feeling, and all negative outcomes, are the result of focusing on what you do not want.

Instead of unconsciously and automatically focusing on what you don't want,

Finding Life's Passion

consciously and intentionally focus on what you do want. When you do this, you instantly begin to create it, and you instantly feel good.

The final characteristic: Happy people are consciously aware. As a result, their brain is less likely run on automatic, creating internal states and internal outcomes they did not intend and do not want.

How do you become more consciously aware? Two ways. The first is meditation. Though traditional meditation is very beneficial, at Centerpointe Research Institute we use an audio technology called Holosync to create deep meditative states, literally at the push of a button. This greatly accelerates the meditation process, and allows you to create increased conscious awareness very quickly.

Second, investigate your own internal processes: your beliefs, values, ways of filtering information, strategies you use for decision making, motivation, and your other internal processes. Centerpointe's Life Principles Integration Process is a structures way of investigating and changing these internal processes, allowing you to take charge of how you create your internal and external results.

There is a price to pay to live the life you love. But paying it is a joyful enterprise, and once you pay it, you will benefit for the rest of your life. So realize that you create your reality, learn to focus your mind on what you want and keep it off of what you don't want, and increase your conscious awareness through meditation and self-inquiry.

The life you love is waiting for you!

Bill Harris

FINDING LIFE'S PASSION

FOUR THINGS I LEARNED FROM FOCUSING ON HELPING OTHERS
Dan Klatt

Before "it" happened for me, almost every day for a year I followed the "Alchemy Process" method that I teach, expanded from Napoleon Hill's book Think and Grow Rich. As part of that process, I decided how much money I wanted to make, by what date, how I was going to make it, and how it would make a difference to others. Day after day for more than a year I impressed my "Alchemy Process Statement" into my subconscious mind. Yet, in my daily work, my mind focused on the thought, "How can I make money?" This was because I had not fully shifted into the part of the process that truly set my intention on fire: "How can I be of greatest service to others?"

The Alchemy Process outcome that I had envisioned was supposed to have occurred by the end of last December. About three days before my deadline, inspiration struck me one morning, just as I woke up. I would create a website, HelpMeMakeOneBillionDollars.com. I would take a group of 144 people through the process of becoming as wealthy as they wanted, even if their goals were to make more than one billion dollars.

To help those 144 become very wealthy, I would focus on two tried and true ideas. The first was Napoleon Hill's, "The Secret," and the second was, "The Carnegie Formula." The same mysterious power that's allowed this to work for me has worked since Biblical times: Give first, and then receive as a result of that difference you've made to others.

After I began my project though, something unexpected happened to me. My outcome evolved. In fact, it took on more universal proportion. When I awoke one morning, the inspiration was 12 times more powerful than before and it hit me like a 24-ton truck. "Hey wait a minute, I can launch the 'ProsperityVirus' and infect people with wealth!" I thought. It would be a complete contrast to the thousands of messages of fear and scarcity that many people are exposed to every day. In that instant, "ProsperityVirus.com: Get Infected!" was born.

I saw that through my expanded awareness rooted in being of greatest service to others I would be able to create a way for many people to break free from "The Matrix of Fear and Limitation (The Real Matrix)" and experience the results of **knowing** they have the power to be as wealthy as they want. Because the Prosperity Virus is so life-changing, people quite naturally want to "Spread The Wealth" and share it with those they care about, and very quickly it becomes a literal Prosperity Epidemic, touching millions of lives!

I have learned four important things. First, I'm very clear about what my life purpose is, and I've dedicated myself to using my natural gifts specifically to help 150 million people become very wealthy. My intention is to help so many people become wealthy the people I help write to thank me for making such a difference to them and their families. I'm honoring the desire within me that needed to find expression through me.

The second thing I learned was that the end result of applying The Carnegie Formula and the Alchemy Process was actually only a stepping stone. It has evolved on its own into the ProsperityVirus which I sense has the Power of Destiny behind it to affect 150 million people very deeply. I had forgotten that the first impulse or destination no matter how powerful it is, as in the case of HelpMeMakeOneBillionDollars.com, is often just the transitional stage leading to your biggest contribution to others.

Third, I learned that when you align your life with purpose and dedicate yourself to it, magic happens. Everything starts flowing smoothly as you become wealthier in all areas of your life. This happens because you're in your flow or, as we say in the East, you're in your "dharma."

Fourth, and most importantly, I learned that life really is all about helping others. I wasn't quite ready for the ProsperityVirus myself until I had mentally committed to helping those 144 people become very wealthy through HelpMeMakeOneBillionDollars.com. The emphasis was on giving people the Key to Riches at a price low enough that even the person most trapped within "The Matrix of Fear and Limitation" could find the way to freedom through this site. It all happened only after I shifted out of "how can I make money" and into "how can I help others;" from "what's in it for me" to "what's in it for you." That transition, which I call the "Consciousness of Wealth," put me in the place of being able to receive the inspiration and gift of the ProsperityVirus.

FINDING LIFE'S PASSION

No matter what your life purpose is, I believe you can take what was transformational for me and apply it to your situation with profound results, following these same four principles:

1. Discover what your life purpose is. This is probably the pursuit you're most passionate about.
2. Recognize that there may be one or more transitional steps. Don't get stuck thinking the first idea is the final idea. Don't limit your results.
3. Align with your life's purpose and stay in the "here and now." Everything will then flow smoothly and your success will come naturally.
4. Your best results come as a result of first helping others.

Start by recognizing that life is all about being of greatest service to others, and ask yourself, "How can I make more of a difference through my deepest passion?" Keep asking that over and over. Because that's the "right" question—it forces your mind to expand to come up with better and better answers. Each new and improved answer you come up with will make more of a difference and be so much more valuable to you, too.

Just to put everything into perspective, think about this: Two days after the third month this year, I had already made more than I had made in all of last year. It makes you realize how "profitable" it is to focus your energy on "what's in it for them."

Dan Klatt

FINDING LIFE'S PASSION

FINDING LIFE'S PASSION

THE OVERNIGHT GOLF PROFESSIONAL
Paula Adelman

At the age of 40, I became a golf professional "overnight." My athletic life began when I was very young. At 10-years-old, I was asked to train for the Olympics in swimming. At 25, I was a tennis professional playing on the Avon Futures Tour. I became a golf professional after I divorced, had a back operation, and moved to Israel with two young children.

As I was growing up my father gave me articles to read about successful women lawyers. His motto was "Once you are a lawyer you can be anything." I always kept that in mind, but I could not give up my love of sports. I believed I could go to law school later but needed to take advantage of the sports opportunities while I was still young.

After we moved to Israel I needed to find a sport that wasn't too hard on my back. I decided to give golf a try. I had been on a golf course only a few times and had played only nine holes each time. The game had seemed boring so I dropped it. But after my back operation I decided to revisit golf.

The first day I arrived at the golf course I spoke to the pro giving a clinic and told him that I was a former tennis professional and was interested in playing golf. During the clinic he asked me to compare one aspect of golf with one aspect of tennis. I answered and then went back to listening. At the end of the clinic an older gentleman introduced himself as Charlie, the head golf professional, and asked if I would like to hit some balls. I said sure, but that I did not really play golf. After hitting about 10 balls he stopped me and said "How would you like to teach with me?" I thought he was joking and again told him that I did not play golf. He responded, "That's ok, I will teach you to teach and play at the same time. I need an assistant to help me with clinics on Fridays." I mentioned that I had two young sons and he said that they could play and learn with the other kids.

Nothing seemed to deter Charlie and his determination for me to consider his offer; and I did consider it. When I returned to the United States in the summer I decided to consult Peggy Kirk Bell, a well-respected golf professional, about this crazy idea. After hitting some balls for her, she gave me her blessing and advised me to, "Go for it."

FINDING LIFE'S PASSION

I returned to Israel, determined to see what this offer was about. When I arrived at the course Charlie greeted me and brought me to the range. I kept shaking my head saying, "This could not really happen to anyone." But it did. I helped him with the clinics on Fridays and he helped me learn the game.

Friday was also the day of the weekly tournaments. I showed up early one day and was asked to fill in for someone. I rushed down the stairs and was greeted by a man who asked me to ride with him. I liked walking and declined his offer. In the middle of the first hole I noticed there was someone in a cart following us. I had not played tournaments before, so I thought he was there to help with scoring. At the end of the hole I asked a man I knew what my partners name was. He said, "Just call him Mr. President." I glanced at the score card and sure enough it read, "Herzog," the President of Israel. I was in a trance from that moment on. I played well, and with my high handicap we ended up winning. Afterward the President asked me to be a regular in their group. He explained that Thomas Friedman, who recently completed research for his book, <u>From Beirut to Jerusalem</u>, just left the country and they needed a fourth person. How could I say no?

There I was, teaching golf on Fridays and playing golf with the President of the country. After four months in this incredible situation I was informed that I could no longer play golf with the President's group. I did not understand. Charlie gave me a weak excuse and I had to tell the President that I needed to teach earlier and could no longer be in the foursome. Later Charlie told me the real reason: Someone had walked into the ladies locker room and asked the president's wife what was between Paula Adelman and the President. His wife didn't want this to hit the newspapers. Charlie said, "Later you can put this in your memoirs."

Charlie told me that, technically, I became a professional golfer on the day I started teaching. I could no longer play in tournaments. As a 20 handicapper I did not understand this. I still had to comply with the rules. For the rest of the year I continued to teach and play. At the end of the year I had a handicap of 10. In the summer, I returned to the United States again with my boys. Unfortunately, the impending Gulf War was in the news and my ex-husband would not allow me to return to Israel with the children.

I was distraught but determined to pursue my golf career. I went to the annual Professional Golf Association (PGA) conference in Nashville, Tennessee, and

FINDING LIFE'S PASSION

befriended a woman who was in the Ladies Professional Golf Association (LPGA). She convinced me to join even though I had played golf for only one year. I got an application, fulfilled all the preliminary requirements, applied, and was accepted as an apprentice.

I needed to play catch-up fast, so I enrolled in the Golf Academy of the South in Orlando. I was the oldest student and one of only two women. In the middle of the semester my friend Joanne, who had advised me to join the LPGA, told me to interview for a teaching job. I revealed my meager golf background to the interviewer, but she hired me anyway.

I spent seven years in Rocky Mount, North Carolina, as the head teaching professional. In 1995 I returned to Israel to start the first golf learning center and range at Wingate Institute. Wingate is the sports institute and college for top athletes. I was a real pioneer and this job turned out to be my dream job. It combined my passion for golf with my interest in Israel.

My golf career started at age 40, my boys became Israel's National Junior Champions and I became a Class A member of the LPGA. My boys were accepted to Ivy League colleges, Harvard and Brown. I am still amazed at all the wonderful experiences I have had as a golf professional. I am living proof that it is never too late to find and follow a passion.

Paula Adelman

Finding Life's Passion

No One Looks Forward to December 26
James A. Sapp

They laughed. "Now, what stupid idea does Jim have?" I can still remember as though it was yesterday; people laughing about a new business I was starting.

The year was 1995, and I had decided to sell vitamins. Shortly after I made this decision, a friend I worked with at Rockwell/Boeing Corporation, Bob Thompson, suggested, "Why don't you market your vitamins on the Internet?"

Have you ever had a light bulb go off in your brain? Well, this was one of those moments.

There was one slight problem: I knew absolutely nothing about the Internet. That seemed, however, like a small speed bump on the road I wanted to travel. My belief was so strong that, even after having invested over 400 hours of work to earn $22, I wasn't discouraged in the least. I had a vision of where I was headed and nothing was going to stop me.

A year and a half later I had more than doubled my income as an engineer with Rockwell Corp.

I had become the first person in my network marketing company to rise to the Diamond level while holding a full time job. Eventually I would walk into my manager's office and resign. I had become one of my company's top distributors because I had a belief that started with a simple seed and grew into a mighty oak.

This was accomplished because I am very good at internet marketing and search engine positioning. However, these achievements are relatively small compared to the promise of my current vision. It is all because of a simple secret I discovered.

As a kid, why did you never have trouble getting up on Christmas morning? There are two reasons: first, you knew that something really good was going to happen to you, and, second, you had an unshakeable belief that there would be presents under the tree. Hence the great excitement and anticipation, creating a great, positive attitude.

Finding Life's Passion

The secret of extraordinary people is that they are excited to get up every day and so should we. By believing something great will happen each day, we bring together unseen forces to help us. This attitude attracts the right people to aid us in accomplishing great things.

Anybody can get excited over something good that's a sure deal–like Christmas. However, what separates the extraordinary from the ordinary is the vision to see what others can't see in the future and take action.

There are two roads in life. One is a very broad, well-paved road and the amazing thing about this road is that you don't have to look for it to find it. By simply doing nothing, it will find you and, in 40 years or less, it will take you to the twin, over-populated cities of Regret and Failure.

On the other hand, there is another road that is much harder to find. It's simply a bare unmarked trail at the beginning, and many people walk past it everyday without noticing. But once in a while it offers a glimpse of the great vision that waits at trail's end.

The great thing about being on this second road is that you meet other travelers who make traveling easier and considerably more fun.

Everyone on this road sees something fascinatingly different "on down the road." Walt Disney saw Disneyland and Epcot Center on this road. Orville and Wilbur Wright could see the future of air travel. Henry Ford could see a nation of automobiles. Our founding fathers could see a land of free men in a country that was the greatest land of freedom and opportunity the world had ever known.

So, if you dare, we invite you to take this "Journey of No Regrets," where the hardest step is always the first.

James A. Sapp

REAL PASSION & INNER STRENGTH
Dr. Aderemi Banjoko

I was brought up in a culture that emphasized education and the importance of becoming a professional. Passions, goals, and ambitions outside that framework were rarely discussed. I became a medical doctor in 1991, specializing in obstetrics and gynecology. For six painful years I pursued goals in that direction. But there was something lacking in my life. I sensed that a higher power was telling me that my real passion lay elsewhere. I began to stumble my way through a journey of discovering who I was and what I was meant to be.

I have discovered that in adulthood you may find that your real passion is not for what you were trained for or what you studied in school. When you then discover what your real passion is and what your heart truly desires, life can get in the way. By that time in my life, I had gone through school, and was stuck in a career that I didn't care for. I was a fully paid, card-carrying member of the rat race with no end to the race in sight. I knew that it would take inner strength and strong faith in a Higher Power to be able to break the chains of "comfort" and take risks, to find my real passion and follow my dreams.

We are sometimes forced by life's circumstances, such as loss of job, bankruptcy, or divorce, to make changes and then find that we are able to follow our real passion and calling in life. My sister is a good example. She trained as a dentist and was working as a dental surgeon when she and her husband moved to where he worked. She was unable to find work as a dentist in Singapore, so she went back to the UK to study health management. During her studies her marriage broke down, despite all efforts. She found that she was unable to obtain employment in health management or in dentistry in the UK. She was broke, unemployed, and had no home. She then started her own business, with no assets. She has become very successful and has helped thousands of people gain employment. She has found her real passion, helping people and changing lives, and that is why she is so successful.

I was inspired by my sister to take a leap of faith and follow God's calling in my life. I have found that my real passion is for helping others succeed and helping orphans and widows in Rwanda. I will now be spending less time in medical practice and more time being an entrepreneur and charity worker. My journey may lead to financial difficulties, setbacks, lack of comfort, and doubts, but I believe that real passion and faith in a Higher Power will see me through!

Dr. Aderemi Banjoko

THE JOY WILL RETURN
Cameron Johnston

Rest at last! My tired body and exhausted brain had been looking forward to this day for months. An extremely busy work year was ending and a well-deserved vacation was beginning. We loaded our two daughters into the car and began a long, unstructured camping trip down the eastern seaboard of the US.

We were less than three hours into this long overdue rest and family adventure when the unpredictable nature of years of poorly managed stress, combined with an overworked and unbalanced lifestyle, called in a long past due account. As I began to relax, an intense depression descended over me that I would not wish on my worst enemy.

For the next three weeks, I did not have a positive thought. My concentration levels were next to zero. I had never felt so hopeless or scared in my life. At the time, I had no idea what was happening or what to do about it.

I learned that because of years of poorly managed stress, my body's energy reserves had been used up. My stress load had exceeded my stress coping ability, and the negative balance had reached overload. As I began to relax, an extreme negative reaction suddenly exploded, and I was in serious depression.

If someone had asked me days before if I felt stressed, I would have said no. Tired, frustrated, in need of rest, yes, but not stressed. Stress can be very deceptive. Therefore, we need to be alert to how stress is affecting us and recognize the stress warning signals. I had been having periodic extreme stress warning signals for years, but went on with life as usual, not realizing the danger just around the corner.

Camping beside the ocean, I often walked along the beach trying to figure out what was happening. One thought kept me sane and brought me through this dark time. Simply trust God. He understands, and he will bring healing and work it all out. Many times a day I prayed, "Lord, I do not know what is happening to me, I cannot think clearly, I can't even pray coherently so I am simply going to relax in you and trust you to see me through this."

FINDING LIFE'S PASSION

With rest, change, support from a loving family and the grace of God, the depression lightened. After two months, I thought that I was ready to go back to work, but within hours of arriving home, I realized I was not ready to go back. I finally went to see my doctor and discovered that I was in the later stages of burnout from which it took me three years to fully recover.

I write this today so that others may avoid an unnecessary experience that can literally derail the most noble of purpose. Stress is the spice of life, but excessive stress, combined with poor coping skills and the unbalanced lifestyle of our 24/7 world, can literally kill you!

I also write to share the good news that full recovery from serious burnout is possible. I speak on *Cooling Off The Stress Soup* and teach skills to develop a stress hardiness needed to enjoy life. I also consult and coach individuals recovering from burnout and bring hope with the good news that a full and complete recovery is possible.

The joy will return.

Cameron Johnston

TURNING POINTS
Jeremy Leming

It was Autumn of 1990, in Augsburg, Germany. As a 20-year-old in the US Army, the last 10 months had been the best of my life. Being stationed in Germany was a dream, and I was taking full advantage of my time there. I was the third person to anxiously sign my name to a list asking for volunteers to go to Kuwait for what would become the "Gulf War." The decision was an easy one, as I was in a military intelligence unit and there was little chance of seeing any real action. I had joined the Army as a teenager, without much direction or purpose in my life. The opportunity in front of me could be my purpose, and I was not about to miss out!

As it turned out, they were taking only 10 people from our unit and in a random draw, my name wasn't picked. Had it been, my life certainly would have taken a different direction. Had I left for Kuwait, it was unlikely that I would have returned to Germany, where I was already dating Conny, the woman who would eventually become my lovely wife. I might have missed the best day of my life–the day my son, Andrew, was born. Sometimes, the things we think we want are simply distractions from the path that leads to our purpose. This was a turning point in my life–one that I didn't control. It put me on the right road.

That road stretched on, without direction it seemed for another nine years. In 1999, I overheard part of a conversation that I had to stop and interrupt. That simple action led to an introduction, an invitation, and eventually a visit to a local canine search and rescue team in Indianapolis, Indiana. Immediately, I was hooked! It was another turning point. The teamwork between dog and handler, the relationship needed to perform at such a high level of competence, and the importance of the task at hand inspired me. I joined the team that day and dove in with all my energy, and ignorance. On the way home I knew that I had found something special. And Conny knew it too. Thankfully, she was patient and understanding enough to support me through time and monetary commitments, disappointments, long hours, and late nights of training.

After failing with my first dog, I got a new puppy, Greif, in the spring of 2001. Shortly thereafter, I joined the Marion County Rescue Task Force, a team designated as FEMA's Indiana Task Force One. I watched as the team deployed on

September 11, 2001, to search the debris of the World Trade Center. I was quite frustrated sitting at home with a puppy, unable to help. I knew that those who were going would perform incredibly, and they did. We are very proud of all those who risked their own lives, "So that others may live."

As my training continued, Greif progressed, and eventually we started going on local searches for missing persons, learning lessons along the way. On August 28, 2005, a call came at about 11:00 pm. Hurricane Katrina was aimed at the Gulf Coast and we were being deployed in advance of the storm. I was not on rotation at the time, but was called as backup because another dog handler was unable to make the trip. This was to be another turning point in my life. Every search is a new situation and you don't know what to expect. You are walking into the unknown and have to deal with what is in front of you. But through the experience we had gained working together, I had complete confidence in Greif. There are many stories to tell about our time in Biloxi, Mississippi. I was quite proud of Greif and the work he did while we were there.

Upon returning to Indianapolis, as is our custom, we all wrote about our experience and the lessons learned on that deployment. Mine included many items about working and training our dogs, dealing with the system, "Thank You's," and other anecdotes. Following is an excerpt that I would like to share with you:

"While I obviously didn't see the media coverage while we were gone, from what I've seen since being back, I think they have largely missed the point. Certainly things went wrong and could have been done more efficiently: but what we saw in Biloxi, besides the destruction, was a vast majority of people who displayed unity and gratitude. I left with a great sense of hope for humanity."

My point is that we may not control all of the external things in our lives, but we certainly control how we perceive them. If you are looking for the negative, you will, without a doubt, find it.

When we returned home, we had a great feeling of satisfaction, not only because we knew we had done a good job, but also because it was an emotional, spiritual, life-changing event. After seeing so many people lose everything–their houses, belongings, family members–but still be so gracious and thankful for the little that we could do, the everyday events that bother us seemed petty. I knew there was going to be a

FINDING LIFE'S PASSION

major change coming. As time passed, life got in the way again. That feeling was gone, and it left an emptiness. Before I realized it, I was focused on the negative, and it was everywhere. Financial troubles, strained relationships of all sorts, and growing dissatisfaction with my job left me with the feeling that I had been to the top of the mountain and had my greatest experience; it was all down hill from here out.

For several years, I had dreamed of starting an organization to help support and train volunteer canine search and rescue teams. Of course, whenever I talked about the idea to someone, they would say, "Oh, that's a great idea, but if it could be done, someone would have already done it." Or even worse, "Who do think you are that you could do that?" Deflated, I allowed those people to put my dream on the back burner. One friend who had just finished telling me every reason why it wasn't possible gave me one important piece of advice. She told me to keep that goal out there where I could still see it, but start working on the small steps that could lead to the dream. That conversation kept the dream alive.

In the seven years I spent as a letter carrier for the United States Postal Service, I can't say I ever really loved the job. My lack of motivation and commitment to the job kept me from doing what I would consider quality work. I was in a rut that seemed endless. The Post Office had paid the bills while I was learning and growing in my passion, but then it simply was in my way! I knew I had to leave the comfortable, beaten path and blaze a trail of my own.

On April 14, 2006, I burned my bridge, sank my ships, and resigned from the USPS. You guessed it: one more turning point, but I chose this one. This might not have been the most reasonable approach, but for me the timing was right. The option for me to bail out of my dream would have been far too tempting when the obstacles started showing up. And they always show up! I had to sink or swim, and the first few strokes were paying the bills. So, I started an internet marketing business. I had it planned out before I left the security of my job, but I was still an absolute beginner. Despite all the hype and claims out there, it is not easy. It was a long, hard process. I have already had some failures and I know there will be more, but the successes have started and I know there will be many more. One thing training dogs taught me is that each failure is an opportunity to learn and to improve yourself. In my short time in the marketing business, I have met many people who just want my money. Fortunately, there are many who are honestly concerned and are willing to help. I decided that my focus would be to help other people to be successful. I had always heard that the best way to get what you want is to help as many people as you can get what they want. After all, helping people is what training search and rescue dogs is all about, so why not build my business on the same principle? The freedom I now have has inspired me and, to my surprise, has provided a level of creativity that I have never experienced in my life. The challenge has been to keep up with my new level of productivity. I see opportunity everywhere I look.

During the same time that I began to follow my real purpose, I started the K9 Search and Rescue Foundation, a nonprofit organization, to help provide support and training to local, state, and national volunteer canine search and rescue teams. The organization will eventually have a training facility to hold seminars and training classes. It will also provide grants and assistance for search gear and equipment. Our foundational principle is to help those who are helping others. I can't think of a better purpose for my life!

Finally, I have started living the life I love. It is a powerful, eye-opening, mind-expanding experience. Instead of holding tightly to everything out of fear of losing it, there seems to be a flow that's constant and increasing. I'm filled with peace knowing that when I fall down, I will get back up and continue. I have found four principles that guide me. I call them the "4 P's": Purpose, Progress, People, and Persistence. "Purpose" is about knowing your passion and never losing sight of it. "Progress," not perfection, is about taking action. Waiting for everything to be perfect in your environment before you act will guarantee failure because it will never happen. Continuous progress allows you to take action one step at a time. "People" means helping others. Regardless of your purpose, relationships are what matter most. "Persistence," is never giving up when you stumble, when people say you can't, or when the hurdle looks too high.

So follow these principles and Wake Up...Live the Life You Love. Here's to our success: yours and mine!

Jeremy Leming

FINDING LIFE'S PASSION

UNIQUE MAGIC
David Kendall

The seed of my dream was planted in 1989 at the age of 21 while traveling the world–Europe and North Africa. But it was in Thailand where I met someone who impacted my life. I met a young man from Chicago who was a professional magician, and I instantly recognized that I wanted to be a magician.

I don't know exactly why because I had never been around the entertainment industry. Standing much less performing in front of people was about as far from my goal as I could possibly imagine. But something called to me, and it would not shut up.

Years later during a detour, I found myself studying education at the University of Victoria, but my burning desire for magic had not subsided. A few years into the program, I knew teaching at least in the educational system was not going to cut it. Inspired by legendary motivational speaker Tony Robbins, I decided to stop wasting my time and pursue my dream of becoming a magician.

Since 1989, I had been practicing and fuelling this magical passion. By the time I gave up on teaching, I was ready to start working as a paid magician. I began with regular gigs in restaurants and pubs while I worked my way into higher pay-ing private and corporate party work.

By 1995 I decided to travel the world with my magic and set off to back to Southeast Asia. After spending some time traveling in Thailand and Nepal, I per-suaded the Westin Stamford Hotel in Singapore to give me a gig performing in venues throughout the hotel.

Not long after, I moved onto Bali, Indonesia and began working with several 5-star resorts.

I moved onto Perth, Australia to begin a whole new chapter in my life. My stay in Australia extended over five years. Not only did I reach heights of success with magic I had never dreamed, but I also met the love of my life and began a family.

A new vision evolved and led our new family back to Canada for yet another new venture. I believe the key to an adventurous life is following your heart. If there is one short formula that has made my life unique, successful and fun, it is constantly asking myself what I want, listening to my heart for the answer and having the guts to follow through–even when it doesn't make a lot of sense.

I believe another key element to living the life you love is just looking around at what everyone else is doing and doing the opposite. This may sound strange, but just try it. You will see the magic in it.

We arrived in Canada in 2000 and I started a personal growth company, Magical Mind Enterprises Ltd. Being a focused individual, this business has turned out to be a financial success and is helping many people in their quest for personal and spiritual growth.

I feel energized and excited everyday knowing that the tools we provide for people are life changing. It's thrilling to know you are helping so many people and at the same time watching my own family grow and prosper and most importantly having the time to spend with my children.

A big part of our mission at Magical Mind Enterprises is helping people wake up and live the life they love and be free. Having freedom and autonomy is in my opinion the real magic of life.

Look after your health. Without great health, energy and vitality, it is difficult to be free and enjoy life.

Be Magical.

David Kendall

A Passion for Giving:
The Anthony Robbins Foundation
Anthony Robbins

Global Impact

The Anthony Robbins Foundation was created in 1991 with the belief system that, regardless of stature, only those who have learned the power of sincere and selfless contribution experience life's deepest joy: true fulfillment. The Foundation's global impact is provided through an international coalition of caring donors and volunteers who are connecting, inspiring and providing true leadership throughout the world!

Global Relief Efforts

The Anthony Robbins Foundation offers its heartfelt compassion to the victims of the numerous natural disasters felt throughout the world. The Foundation is passionate about participating in the coordination of reconstruction activities and evaluates funding requests on an ongoing basis. As men and women affected by these disasters begin to rebuild, the Anthony Robbins Foundation takes honor in providing hope and funding support to the many suffering communities.

Adopt-A-School Program, New Orleans, USA

Katrina Relief Efforts continue to be a focus of the Foundation. The Foundation will support the rebuilding efforts throughout the Gulf Coast through a partnership with its Youth Mentoring Program partner, Communities In Schools (CIS). CIS is the nation's leading community-based stay-in-school network, connecting needed community resources with schools. CIS has over thirty-four chapters serving well over 2 million children nationally. The Foundation will focus on rebuilding the educational infrastructure currently affecting thousands of children in Louisiana, Mississippi, and Alabama.

The Foundation is proud to announce its partnership with the Adopt-A-School Program in New Orleans to support the rebuilding efforts of Ben Franklin Elementary. This elementary school was the first public school to open in New Orleans post-Katrina. Ben Franklin Elementary is operating near its capacity by serving 555 students, a 24% increase in student population since Hurricane Katrina. Over 90% of its students reside in high poverty households. The

FINDING LIFE'S PASSION

Foundation will provide funding and hands-on assistance toward rebuilding the library, playground and other structural needs. The Foundation's goal is to provide the funds and tools necessary to transform this elementary school into an enhanced learning environment.

Adopt-A-School Program, The Citizens Foundation, Pakistan

The Anthony Robbins Foundation will provide support to The Citizens Foundation which manages many relief programs in Pakistan, rebuilding schools and homes following the earthquake on October 8, 2005. It is widely recognized that, because of crumbling schools, the children suffered the greatest blow from the October quake. It has been reported that some 10,000 schools collapsed throughout Pakistan. The Anthony Robbins Foundation is proud to support the construction of a 6500 square foot school in the Bagh district of Kashmir, Pakistan. Upon completion, this school will serve 180 students during the academic year beginning in April 2007.

Hebron Orphanage, India

Over the past 40 years, Hebron Orphanage has saved homeless orphans from dying of starvation on the streets of southern India. These orphaned children have been given love, life and a future. The Anthony Robbins Foundation adopted Hebron Orphanage following the 2004 Tsunami. The orphanage has expanded its facilities and now accommodates 400 children. The Foundation is delighted to provide funding to support Hebron Orphanage's immediate need to build a new stand-alone boy's dormitory, enabling the number of male residents to increase to 100, and to allow the current boy's dormitory to be used as a library and classrooms.

Langfang Children's Village, Beijing China

The Langfang Children's Village in Beijing, China was founded to support mainland China's orphaned and special needs children. Many children come to the village because they are abandoned at the front gates or brought to the Langfang by locals. It is home to more than 90 orphans from approximately ten different orphanages scattered throughout China. China is working hard at improving the plight of these children, but as a developing country with over 5 million orphans, the problem is simply too large.

The Langfang Children's Village is designed to model a normal family environment and de-emphasizes the institutional feel often associated with orphanages. Every child lives in a freestanding home with house parents and their own yard to play in. The Anthony Robbins Foundation provides funding to the Langfang Children's Village to support the daily needs of the children as well as medical treatment at an on-location clinic. This collaborative effort is contributing to the well-being of these beautiful children, allowing the Foundation to work toward fulfilling its mission of global impact.

Global Community Connection Day
The Anthony Robbins Foundation proudly sets aside one day a month to proactively connect with non-profit organizations throughout the world. Its goal is to meet the challenges of a global community, come up with solutions and TAKE ACTION! We visit and provide in-kind donations to schools, hospitals, and shelters for the homeless to nurture, feed and mentor those in need. Recently, the Foundation supported the Children's Hospitals of San Diego and New Orleans with donations of stuffed bears for their in-patients. The Foundation also supported the Diabetes Association in their annual Tour de Cure cycling event held in San Diego and Santa Monica, California in honor of the National Physical Fitness and Sports Month.

Anthony Robbins

FINDING LIFE'S PASSION

THE MOST IMPORTANT THING!
Kimberly Mac

O ne of the most important things in life is to love what you do. When you are living what you are truly passionate about, life seems like a dream. You can work 18 hours a day, and it doesn't feel as if any time has passed. When you love something, all time stops, there are no limits and you are present in the moment. That is living life! Or is it?

I was in love with my job in every way. My life seemed perfect, except for one thing. I didn't have a life outside of my job, creating an imbalance that, over time, creates illness. Balance is essential for health and longevity.

In August of 1994, I learned the importance of balance when I was suddenly stricken with a debilitating illness; I was not even able to walk. For nine and a half months I was in the dark, in the hands of dozens of doctors who had no idea of what was wrong or what my body needed. I was helpless and in excruciating pain, and did not know whether I would ever walk or even stand on my own again. I thought, "Why me?" I would think about all the things I had always wanted to do, but never did. I would think about death and what it meant. What would I do if I knew that I was dying? How would I live if I knew that I was dying? I realized that I would not be living the way that I had been living.

This illness gave me a chance for a new life, even if I didn't know it at that time.

The doctors inadvertently had given me a challenge with their diagnosis of the incurable disease, Fibromyalgia, and their remedy of medication everyday for the rest of my life. Drugs and their incurable diagnosis would rule my life. I decided I would be in control.

These are the key steps I took in order to regain my health and my life. I believe these are essential to living a healthy life with purpose.

Step #1: Belief that I could heal by my own will.

Nothing is going to be in control of me. Taking a stand for myself was my first step to healing. My belief in my own ability to heal myself started me on a journey to healing with my intuition as my guide.

We have choices: the choice to choose the life we desire to live, the life we are meant to live or we choose not. Either way, we choose.

Step #2: Awareness and recognition of the power of things when they are given to me.

It took some years to understand the reason why I had Fibromyalgia. I believe that I was given a gift in having this illness. As a result, I was guided to take control of my own destiny. It stopped me from using everyone and everything as an excuse not to live the life that I was meant to live. Since I appeared to be the healthiest person everyone knew, it was a shock that I, of all people, would be ill. With this, I understood my power in having Fibromyalgia was to teach others how to make health their priority.

Step #3: Decide and take action for what I want.

I decided that I would be in control of my health for the rest of my life. This decision was what led me to cure myself of Fibromyalgia. Holistic health education became my primary focus, followed with active steps for real results. As I learned, health does not remain if you fail to take action to keep it.

Living healthy is my key to youth and longevity. Without health, all the money, family, friends and time means nothing since you can't enjoy them.

Know the power you have inside you. You can achieve anything you desire. Just believe in yourself. Follow your belief with passion, education and action to get everything you want in life.

Kimberly Mac

LIFE AFTER TRAGEDY
Benjamin F. Bostic

I had worked in construction for nearly 15 years before my accident. Each day was different and the work was good. But one day in autumn changed everything. On November 29, 2000, I went to work to operate a backhoe in Ridgefield, Connecticut. I was in my foreman's truck, sitting in the front passenger side. The company flatbed truck driver was in his truck doing paperwork. We pulled in front of him, leaving a six–eight–foot gap between the trucks. I got out, and the driver and I exchanged waves. Then, I heard a loud bang!

At that point, I was between both trucks, and I saw a worker running up the hill waving his hands. Then I saw the grill of the flatbed truck coming toward me. I tried to get out of the way, but there wasn't time. I closed my eyes and, "Bang!" I was pinned between both trucks. The force of the runaway wreck dragged me about sixty feet and I found myself lying beside one of those trucks. I tried to get up, but all I felt was pain everywhere. I thought I was moving, but I wasn't. I tried again. Finally, my co-worker, Mark, came to my rescue. I knew I was in trouble. My right leg was mangled and there was blood everywhere. Mark tied a belt around my leg to help stop the bleeding and stayed with me until an ambulance arrived. I lost consciousness on the ride to the hospital.

When I woke up, I was in the ICU. In the room with me were my twin brother, Bernard, my younger brother, Tyrone, my parents, Edward and Magnolia, my sister Cynthia, and my daughters, who were only twelve and ten. Normally, they don't let that many people in the ICU, but they gave us a few minutes. My entire body was swollen and I had a collapsed lung and six broken ribs.

A few days later, the doctor told me that they had amputated my right leg. Because of all the medication I was taking, I didn't comprehend what he had said. One day, as I was sitting up, I looked down, and noticed that my leg was gone from mid-thigh down! I became very upset, so my doctor explained it to me once again. He said that my leg had been mangled from the knee down, but because of infection from lying in the dirt, they had to amputate above my knee.

FINDING LIFE'S PASSION

The remainder of my hospital stay was very difficult. I was angry and upset. I worried about the future and I couldn't sleep. I lost my temper and lashed out at those who were trying to help me, including my family, and my daughters, Maryssa and Cassandra.

When I was well enough, I was moved to Gaylord Rehabilitation Hospital in Wallingford. After only two weeks, I was discharged. I started outpatient care at Gaylord Rehab Center in New Haven, where I learned to walk with my prosthetic leg. For motivation, I looked at photographs of my girls. I was determined to get my life back. There were times when my leg would buckle or fall off. I'd just laugh it off and stumble back into the house to put it back on. I realized how important it was for me to keep trying and never give up.

Eight months after the accident, I went back to work, strictly as an operator, and then I ran a portable material plant. One day I twisted my left ankle, but I didn't tell anyone. I thought it would heal on its own, but it didn't. I went for treatment twice a week for six weeks, but it didn't help. An MRI showed a torn tendon. My doctor said that I needed surgery. My good ankle needed surgery and I was going to be laid up for three months.

I had also been laid off from work and did not wish to return. I decided to start a home business.

I know there are lots of people who would worry about starting a business under those conditions, but I am not one of them. After all, life had already taught me that a missing limb could be overcome; that predictions about never working again could be proven false and that the worst fears imaginable could be turned into hope for the future.

The lesson is clear to me: as long as I stay focused on the things that matter, just as I did in rehabilitation, anything is possible. As long as the image of my daughters is clearly in front, I will be able to draw all the strength, courage and inspiration that I need. It is our passion to succeed that can carry us over insurmountable obstacles and right through impenetrable barriers.

If you cannot believe in yourself, then you can believe in the beauty of your family, or the worthiness of your objective. Believe in the need of others, or the power of your dream to make a better world. As long as you have a pulse, you can have a passion, and that passion will save your life.

Benjamin F. Bostic

HAVING A PASSION FOR THE MASTERY OF LOVING!
Matthew G. Sikich II

I became a personal and family dynamics consultant and the developer of the "Mastery of Loving" Relationship Course due to my own personal life experiences. The trials and challenges in my life have fueled my desire and passion to help others in creating lasting and loving relationships in their lives.

Dr. Robert Schuller, a gifted man who is called "Minister of the Good News of Jesus Christ," says, "With God you can turn your scars into stars!" Looking back, I can see clearly how "our Creator" has orchestrated people and events to lead me through trials and challenges to my passion and purpose.

Growing up, I realized my parents, however well-intentioned in their own minds and hearts, fell short of understanding and providing for my own individual needs, as a child, to receive love in a meaningful fashion. At the age of 12, a spiritual experience led me to know deeply and completely Jesus' personal message to love one another.

My brother Mike was killed the day before Christmas Eve in 1970 while serving in Vietnam. We were extremely close, and I loved him very much. In my extreme hurt, I chose to be angry at our Creator and turned away from Him. Through this time in my life, I did keep the personal message of love toward others (that His Son gave me) alive in my heart. Little did I realize then; our Creator kept loving me even though I had chosen not to love Him.

The result came in 1988 when my daughter, who is extremely special to me, was born. Participating completely in the creation of a life was wonderful, spiritual, and powerful; it made me realize the awesome presence of a Creator of all life. I assisted in delivering my daughter in a water birth. She came out of her mother's womb into my very hands! Being a father to this tiny infant and watching her grow drew me closer to understanding there was indeed a Father of us all, and there are natural ways that we can be safe and secure in His hands!

He began to reveal to me how He would use and direct me to help enhance and restore marriages, to bring more joy, peace and love into anyone's relationships, whether they are single, parents, children, friends, co-workers or even strangers. I became very serious and passionate about this work that our Creator had called me to, because of the enormous need in today's society. In the last two years, I have been directed by Him to expand The "Mastery of Loving" Relationship Course on a national and international basis. I once asked Him, "Why did You choose me?" At the time, I was going through a "Moses" experience–feeling uneasy about being called to publicly bring this information to the masses. He answered, "Because you listened, and you cared."

"The Mastery of Loving" Program is now available to those who desire a unique and complete understanding and practicality of how we can love ourselves and others more, and on purpose. We are translating the program into other languages to help even more people.

Romans 8:28 says, "We know that in everything God works for good with those who love him, who are called according to his purpose." This fuels the passion everyday in my life!

Matthew G. Sikich II

THERE'S MORE TO THE PICTURE THAN MEETS THE EYE
Denise M. Lynn

D o you remember in grade school when you found out that you weren't a superhero and you couldn't do everything? Perhaps you couldn't play baseball or you were a poor speller. Mine was art.

I will never forget the day my third grade teacher, Ms. Debilious, said, "Clear your desks. We're going to do an art project." I was excited! I loved colors, paints and the feel of paper. I loved art and I was ready to explore my creative side. In kindergarten I was a very happy finger-painter. Ms. Debilious got us set up in the room and told us to turn to the person on our right and draw their profile.

I was mortified. No colors, only drawing. I raised my hand in protest. I told her I thought there would be colors. She told me to be quiet. I was so upset. I let the girl to my right go first. She took her time studying my profile. She held her pencil up in that "measuring the perspective" way professional artists have. I got more and more nervous sitting there thinking about how was I going to do it–I didn't know how to draw! After 30 minutes Ms. Debilious announced that it was time to switch. It was my turn. My 30 minutes began.

I looked at the paper. It just didn't come out of me. I drew a line and erased; then drew another and erased. Then another line was created and erased. Time seemed to go on forever. The bell rang for the five-minute warning and I still had only three lines on the paper with something that may have resembled an eye. Ms. Debilious called time and it was over.

The next part was even worse. We had to stand in front of the class in pairs to show our drawings. My partner had a perfect rendition of my profile. She found herself apologizing for my slightly upturned nose. Everyone praised her for the likeness of me, even with my nose. Then it was my turn. At first I just wasn't going to show it. Ms. Debilious said, "Denise, you have to show your work or you will not get a grade for this assignment. You know you can't afford that." Great! Now everyone knew I wasn't doing well. When I finally turned my paper around, everyone laughed. The profile didn't look like my partner at all. It looked like a cross between a stick figure and a clown with a missing eye. I made a decision right then and there I was never going to draw in public again and I most certainly was never going to be an artist.

From grade school to high school I never took a class in art again. I had one teacher who let us do pictures of our dreams. She called them "mendalas." I enjoyed the abstract use of colors with no judgment as to the meaning and use of the design. We got to interpret our dreams through art. It was great. One day the teacher told me she thought I should take an art class, because of my passion for the mendala work. I only laughed and gave her my patent answer, "But I don't draw."

My mother loves museums and art, so I spent a lot of time looking at art with awe. I admired and could see the brilliance of Monet and Renoir, my favorite artists. But I knew there wasn't going to be some miracle that would bring out my creative side. I was Salieri to Mozart. I could feel it, understand it, and know what it meant to love art, but I was never going to be an artist.

Life went on. I was lucky and found my purpose in life very young. By my thirties I was a successful mover-and-shaker in my healing consulting business. Clarity Consulting was familiar to people in the know and I was happy that I had found my purpose. I felt great helping people realize their dreams. I was respected as the healers' healer. I had a sense of accomplishment and knew I was really making a difference.

Then it happened. One day I was doing a session on a client like any other day. She told me about her daughter, who was in art school getting her Master's Degree. We finished the session on a great note and she left. While I was driving home, I realized that I was really upset. I was full of road rage, which isn't hard to do in Los Angeles, but I knew there was something wrong. I pulled over and thought, "What is going on with me?" I thought about my day, but didn't find anything that would have bothered me, so I cleared my thoughts and went about my evening.

The next time I worked with that same client she asked me about an idea her daughter had for her final art project. There was a tree that was to be a symbol of life. I had an idea about how the project could be used as a political statement communicating the process of how Church and State had been used during the aftermath of September 11, 2001. My opinion was quickly rejected. She said that it just wouldn't be her daughter's style. This time when our session was over, I was even more upset. I thought the problem was that I felt rejected because my idea

Finding Life's Passion

was tossed aside and maybe I wasn't really in touch with what this client needed. I thought she may need to work with someone new.

Later, this same client told me about her daughter winning a fellowship to paint for the summer. I couldn't believe my reaction. I thought I would die it hurt so much! I sat in my office and cried. I knew this client needed to work with someone else. I was clearly not able to help her any more. Why was I getting so upset over an art student? I wasn't an artist; I was a healer. My purpose was to help people become clearer about their lives, not to be a frivolous artist. I even had a statement about my purpose. I had been trained to remember who I am. I repeated out loud several times, "My purpose is to provide clarity and encouragement with loving insight to help people achieve their life's dreams." I knew who I was. My mission was clear and there wasn't anything that would change my mind.

Never say never. It happened on a Sunday, of all days. I was taking a dance class that I affectionately called "dance church" or "sweat your prayers." The idea of the class is to be connected to God in reflection by free-style dance meditation. Music is played in five rhythms and you go through the stages of sound from calm to chaos and back to calm without speaking. As I danced I thought about my week.

I was very connected to what had happened with my client with the art student daughter. I was wondering how I was going to tell her that I needed to find her a new consultant. The music changed again to chaos and the room erupted. It was perfect. I was stomping on the ground feeling very connected to anger and to the chaos around me. The pain and the anger of the week was bubbling up like a volcano. I was sweating and having a good cry when somehow I stopped and looked up. I saw a wonderful ray of sunlight pouring into the room from the skylight. As I followed the light down I saw a very tall man under the light and something me inside said, "Go paint him in his essence." In all of the chaos I still heard my mantra, "You can't paint. You have to know how to draw and you can't draw." But this time something was different. With the drumbeat in the background I heard something else, "It doesn't matter if you can't draw. Go paint." The music had changed and calm had returned to the room. I knew what I had to do. I left the class right then and the next I knew, I was in the art store buying paints, canvas, brushes, and everything you could think of.

I painted and painted and painted. I copied my favorite paintings by Monet and Renoir on the walls of my apartment. Of course they didn't look like the masters, but at some moments I saw the essence. I kept painting. I bought books on how to paint and I took classes. I ruined the carpet in my apartment, but I didn't care. I was painting. It became clear to me that I had found a passion.

I began to paint with even more passion and purpose. The question was, how was I going to get my paintings to the public? I wondered whether anyone would buy my work.

One day I called a friend, Scott Komie, who had owned a fine art gallery. When he arrived, quietly he looked around. We chatted about everything but the art work all over my house. Then he carefully began to study my paintings. He told me to write numbers like 375, 750, and even 1500. When I asked him what these numbers were, he said that they were the sale prices. He was impressed with my work and told me that I needed to do a show.

I found a location and started to work. Almost everyone I knew helped. My parents handled food and beverages, my brother helped with the photos, my friends helped with my hair and clothes.

On October 26, 2002, I had my first one-woman art show titled, More to the Picture Than Meets the Eye. I exhibited 56 paintings and 65 people attended. The night was magical. One last guest came in at the end of the evening. After a few moments, I realized that he was my accountant. He looked around and complimented my work. Then he pointed to three different pieces and said that he wanted to buy them. In total, I sold five pieces that night and after the show I felt like a whole new world had opened for me. I had found my passion.

Four years later, I am still consulting and still have my client with the art student daughter. My artwork hangs in people's homes, bringing them joy and happiness. I have done another show and I have my own website. I have been published in an international book and have a working studio in Beverly Hills. I have sold more than 35 pieces. I plan to keep going.

I discovered that you can have both a passion for something and a purpose in the same lifetime. I was lucky to have found both. I am an actual artist who still can't draw.

ᢙ *Denise M. Lynn*

FINDING LIFE'S PASSION

NEVER GIVE UP!
Brian D. Fiske III

Ten years ago I had a difficult decision to make. To this day I believe it was probably the most difficult in my life.

My two daughters had moved to Los Angeles with their mother from our home in Boston. After a year of visiting my children, who were still young, I decided that I needed to live closer to them. The distant relationship was breaking my heart. Leaving my family and friends in Boston and moving 3000 miles away, not knowing a single soul in Los Angeles or having a job, was a difficult gamble, to say the least.

After driving cross-country for a week, I arrived in L.A. I moved into a small apartment and, after unpacking my small van, the reality of my move soon unfolded. Although I was thrilled to be with my children again, my decision soon became a nightmare. My goal of quickly finding a job seemed to evaporate quickly and I wasn't able to find a position in healthcare. With no family or friends close by for support, I soon became very depressed. I realized I might have to return to Boston. I would have to leave my two children again.

It was at this point in my life that I reflected on my accomplishments as well as failures. I had originally graduated from college with a B.S. in Aviation Management as well as my Commercial Pilot's license. I had been a flight instructor and aviation had been my passion! Unfortunately, the economy of the early 1990s found me unemployed in the aviation field and I entered the healthcare field as a social worker to be able to support my young family. I thought my dream of being successful in the aviation field had ended. When I had worked with the elderly as a social worker, I remember many of my patients telling me how quickly their lives had passed. Many of them regretted not pursuing their dreams and told me not to give up on my passion to stay in the aviation field.

I decided to stay in Los Angeles, and I accepted a position as a manager with a fast-food restaurant to pay the bills. I was happy to be with my children, but I was miserable every day when I went to work. I was depressed and I knew I had to make a change. In my off-time I studied and earned my real estate license. Then a

FINDING LIFE'S PASSION

colleague introduced me to some personal development books. After I devoured the first two books which included *As a Man Thinketh* by James Allen and *Think and Grow Rich* by Napoleon Hill, it seemed as though I had awakened from a life-long coma. Although I was already an educated person, personal development tapes and books began to open new doors to a new chapter in my life. I have never looked back. My passion and love had been the field of aviation. I knew I had to get back into that business and so I started my quest to find a position even if it meant not flying as a pilot. I visited airports all over southern California and I soon got my break. I and was hired by a premier private jet charter company in Van Nuys as a flight coordinator, arranging flights all around the world for successful people and celebrities.

My commute to my new job was an hour each way or more, with the L.A. traffic. I soon found that listening to self-development programs made the commute a pleasant way to travel. Listening to dozens of those programs gave me incentive to accelerate at work. I began to be promoted to higher positions. I also pursued my Master's degree in Aviation Management, a goal I had given up years ago. Soon after returning to aviation I earned the opportunity to become Vice President for a growing company in Las Vegas.

I was able to assist in the growth of this company, which is now one of the larger charter companies on the West Coast. My continuing passion for self-development in the field of aviation found me interacting with some of the biggest celebrities in Hollywood, as well as some of the most successful business people in the world. By simply becoming a goal-oriented person and using the tools I acquired from self-development, I changed my life!

After several years of living in Los Angeles, I moved to the fast-growing Inland Empire located between San Diego and Palm Springs to be closer to my children. I have since earned my Master's degree with Embry-Riddle Aeronautical University and I teach graduate school as a part-time instructor. I am also an executive for a new private jet charter company, continuing in my passion for aviation. I have recently started pursuit of a Ph.D. with the goal of becoming a success coach teaching others how to overcome life's obstacles.

There is no doubt that life can throw you a curveball at anytime. Ten years of my life were filled with uncertainty. Personal development materials allowed me to set a direction for my life, and I was able to achieve the goals that I had previously given up. I am grateful to those elderly patients of mine who reflected on their lives and reminded me not to lose my passion. Many of those wonderful people had given up their dreams only to find themselves trapped in aging bodies, angry that they had given up hope early in life. Our time on this earth is a short ride with limited opportunity to achieve our passions. Start today and knock down the barriers that block your path to success. Set goals and work hard to reach them. By becoming a student of personal development and helping others do the same, you will be able to live the life you love with passion!

Brian D. Fiske III

CELEBRATE YOUR EXISTENCE, FOR IT IS YOUR PRIVILEGE!
Shirley Cheng

D o you love life unconditionally? Do you accept and cherish days that are dark and dreary? Does your passion for life die away when life seems to play games which you lose? It is easy to love life when you achieve what you desire; you embrace life when things go right. But what if life throws stones when you least expect it? How do you feel when life seems to turn its back on you? If, as I did, you suddenly lost eyesight, would you still feel passionate and continue to see past your loss and look into a bright future, and cherish the privilege of what you had in the past?

I love life unconditionally, and the flames of my passion will never die. I know, too, that life loves me unconditionally in return. But how, you must wonder, could I believe that life loves me unconditionally, when it has snatched my eyesight away, leaving me to yearn for sight of the stars that I can now only wish upon?

For my first seventeen years I had the honor of beholding the beauty of our world. I experienced the sheer pleasure of seeing my mother's smile alight upon her eyes. I delighted in treating my soul to the breathtaking scenes of nature–the celestial diamonds, the green velvet that blankets our Earth, and the glistening mirrors that winter creates upon our ponds. I have lovingly tucked these photographs in my mind, and I am still able to enjoy them in my heart, from which I continue to see the world. I do not scorn life for taking away my ability to see; instead, I am grateful for having owned this power before.

When you fall in love with someone, are you falling in love with a perfect person? No, because that person does not exist. Instead, you love that person for who he or she is and how he or she makes you feel. Thus, with life, acknowledge the times you have lost and be grateful for what you have won. And unlike an imperfect lover, life will never abandon you; for better, for worse, for richer, for poorer, in sickness or in health, the sun rays will never leave your side.

Knowing this, I am passionate about being alive and returning life's love with an intensity that matches the power of fire. My heart dances whenever I think about my existence.

Finding Life's Passion

What does it mean to be alive? Being alive is having the privilege to smile, to laugh, to taste, and to touch. It is having the ability to smell the special scent your mother carries, to run with the wind, and to dance with your heart.

Without life, how could you have known the delight of waking up to the songs of birds or dancing to the rhythm of the ocean? How could you have seen the beautiful arch across the sky after a refreshing rain? And how could you have the chance to taste your salty teardrops on your lips?

Our lives give us other priceless treasures as well. We have a full spectrum of emotions; the sharing of feelings; our talents, ideas, and imagination; and countless of other riches of the universe. We are indeed immeasurably rich, much richer than the infinite unborn souls.

True, not all the jewels our existence has given us will shine and shimmer; many of them are steep mountains we must climb and deep oceans we must cross, but these challenges and obstacles are the jewels that make us stronger. Challenges are life's vaccines: they exercise your spirit to help you withstand high winds and equip your soul with the necessary tools to battle future storms.

I have received many of these vaccines; the obstacles have left numerous scars on my body in all shapes and sizes, but these marks have made me stronger and more invincible as I wait for the next high mountain to climb. I relished the taste of victory each and every time I battled and won. If there were no challenges, how could I name myself a victor? If there were no darkness, how could the stars appear so bright?

Be thankful for the gems that sparkle; focus on the gifts your existence has bestowed upon you. Do not let any dust or dirt tarnish the value of these diamonds; the dirt itself cannot touch or harm the treasures–only you have the power to ultimately soil the gems, so handle them with grace and appreciation. For each day that passes, thank for that day and its riches. Instead of waiting for a disaster to strike to be thankful for what little is left after its devastation, love and appreciate everything and everyone right now.

I embrace my existence with my whole heart and soul, and I accept all the jewels–the bright, along with the not-so-bright–my life has granted me. I cherish

Finding Life's Passion

my existence and everything else it encompasses, knowing that I can create more wondrous treasures by using what I have. Although I'm blind, I can see far and wide as my heart tells me all it sees; even though I'm disabled, I can climb high mountains, for my spirit soars with the wind, unafraid to face any rain and hail. In spite of all the high mountains I have had to climb, I have arrived at each and every top with a smile. I have conquered thorny jungles and fiery seas and come out with stars in my arms. I am able to achieve all this, for I count my blessings every day, knowing that there is always someone out there who is in a much worse situation than I am in, so I am thankful for what I have and who is around me.

Some souls have let their troubles veil the gems, so they have been unable to treasure the diamonds. Do not let the same misfortune happen to you. When you are given life, hold on to it tightly yet delicately; cherish what has been given to you: your privilege to enjoy dawn's first rays, your power to give words of comfort to a stranger, and your fortune to receive warm embraces after a good cry. If you allow your mishaps to cloud these treasures–or do not realize the true value of challenges–you will make your situation worse than it already is, losing every good thing you do have. And watch out for the thieves who try to belittle your gifts; they are the people who refuse to recognize the worth of life.

What would you have missed if your existence had never existed?

I know I am able to laugh; I am able to weep. Without my life, I would be able to do none of these. Thus, let us celebrate our existence together and return life's unconditional love; let us rejoice the beauty of our treasures, and embrace all of our days!

Shirley Cheng

Finding Life's Passion

LIVING WITH PASSION
W. Patrice Martin

When I was 22, a young man entered the New American newspaper building where I was working and told me that I had a mission to fulfill. He said I was to "Please relate the truth."

I was very excited by his words, as I had no idea about my destiny or what I was suppose to be doing with my life. Later, I found out that he had escaped from a mental institution. I sadly dismissed what he said because, well, he was "crazy." However, as my life began to unfold it became clear that my destiny was indeed tied to the discovery of truth and how we are to live it. After years of study and experience I have begun teaching what I have learned. I have decided to consciously live my truth and my destiny with passion.

I am the creator, designer and promoter of the Spiritual Healing in Feeling and Thought (SHIFT) Movement. It is the model that I use to teach Life Skills. I like to refer to it as "life skills on steroids." I teach the skills that help people live more productive lives by setting goals, managing time, making quality decisions and changing self-defeating attitudes. But I go deeper into what life is really all about. I examine the age old questions: What and who am I? Where did I come from? Where am I going? Why am I here?

I have narrowed the scope of my destiny to a spiritual vision. This vision focuses on the revitalization of impoverished minds and communities. It is about uplifting the inner and outer experiences of people who are in bondage and plagued with thoughts and feelings of hopelessness. It is about setting the captives free.

Think of me as the Harriett Tubman of the new shift in consciousness toward which this planet is moving. I am going back for my people. I am unplugging them from the matrix system that is truly on the way out. In truth it is time for us all to shift and create our own reality; our new and improved lives.

I am a part of a larger network of people who share a similar vision. We have a holistic approach to meeting the needs of these impoverished communities. All of our individual work/play is designed to promote peace and prosperity.

FINDING LIFE'S PASSION

I start by changing the way people see themselves and empowering them with the truth of who they are as spiritual beings: people made in the likeness and image of the creator with the same abilities and power to create their own reality

I teach them and demonstrate that the life they have is the life they have created through the thoughts they think, the emotions they feel, the words they speak and the actions they take on a daily basis.

As I work to renew and enlighten minds, others work to make people feel good about themselves by showing them how to live healthy and fit lifestyles. People are also taught about managing their finances and investing. The first investment they are encouraged to make is in a home of their own. There are advisers already in place to see people through this process from beginning to end. All along the way, I teach the importance of a "Millionaire Mindset" because it is clear that this country is moving away from having a middle class. There will be the rich, the working poor, and the poor. Although it is upon the poor and working poor that I have placed my attention, I don't intend to leave anyone out. There are many people I want to help grasp the truth of who we are, regardless of race, religion, ethnic background or gender.

I am especially moved to embrace my fellow "baby boomers." I have a special love for my generation. We were so bold and idealistic; many of us still are. Unfortunately it is often difficult to figure out what to do or where to start because the issues we face feel so overwhelming.

Most of us may be comfortable, but not wealthy. When I speak to members of this group I find that some aren't at all interested in accumulating wealth for themselves, let alone wealth to leave to their families. It is also apparent that they aren't into mastering self development if it's too painful. Spiritual concepts are rooted in "that old time religion" that is good enough for them, yet it doesn't seem to be transforming their world on the inside or the outside. They take their cues from the preacher who is the flavor of the month without doing the personal study that leads to personal revelation directly from spirit itself.

I would like very much to open a dialogue with my peers about the ideas surrounding the nature of the universe, the laws that govern our reality and how they are put in place to make sure we live a happy and abundant life.

So I submit for your edification the S.H.I.F.T Movement. We plant into the foundational spiritual ground of impoverished (rich and poor) people the seeds of healing (physical, mental, emotional, and spiritual) and a new thought about who they can be through the love and passion of the creator of all that is.

The vision I hold for enlightenment and peace on this planet is not a delusion. I see parents learning and growing, and teaching the children in safe places of abundant living created by their own renewed minds.

Welcome to a new way of seeing and believing. Much love and peace.

W. Patrice Martin

THE LONG HAUL
Ed Rust

To prepare for the future we, as human beings, need a sense of history. This is how we learn; how we grow. Learning from the past enables us to focus on our purpose–driving our future.

From the beginning, everyone has enormous potential. It is a matter of life and what you do with the experiences you face.

When dealing with "learning experiences," we must look at the overview–the big picture. When facing an obstacle, it must be looked at with caution by asking these questions: Is it hard to overcome? Will it slow me down? Am I looking at the obstacle as a pessimist or optimist? Can I go around the obstacle like I would a mountain? Can I break it down into pieces? Is it really an obstacle at all?

If you read an obstacle the wrong way, that's okay. You can't be embarrassed about honestly saying, "Hey, I messed up." The most important thing to remember is you can't take yourself seriously, but you must take your responsibilities with all seriousness.

Experiences give us character. They make us who we are. I was lucky to have had a unique experience with State Farm. When I first began my career, my managers took time to mentor me by teaching me from their experiences. Their example taught me how to be a great boss–a great mentor. Three broad principles emerged: First, you may not execute your philosophy as well as you like, but you can voice your advice about the details. Second, you can be successful by surrounding your-self with the "best people for the job." Finally, you must let your employees do their jobs–let them run and develop their own experiences.

If you have advice about the details, be a coach asking the right questions in a non-threatening manner. Touch what is on people's minds and in their hearts. Give credit away; don't keep it for yourself. Let others know what a great job they are doing. Be a teacher, a cheerleader–not a rule-giver or a jailer.

It is a great mistake to assume the world is the same today as it was 10 years ago.

FINDING LIFE'S PASSION

Do listen to your intuition about the "changing world," but don't forget to ask, "Am I reading the world correctly?"

To make the long haul of life, discover your passion. Be willing to be a student of this; then, be willing to be a teacher. Open your experiences to others. We all make the wrong turn somewhere, this is the crazy experience we call, "life." When teaching, don't forget to be a coach not a lecturer.

It is your purpose to help others find and keep their passions. Do it with understanding; do it with your own passion.

Ed Rust

Thank God I Was Disabled
Scott McClure

I was 26-years-old, on the fast track to success and in the prime of my life. Then disaster struck. I had grown up in the small town of Tyler, Texas, where I attended Tyler Junior College and then the University of Texas at Austin. I landed my dream job in marketing management with Nestlé in Los Angeles. After working hard for many years, I was managing a $170 million brand and was destined for upper management. I owned my own home, dated beautiful women, and was achieving things I had never dreamed were possible in the past. By all standard measures, I was successful.

Then, I began to feel ill. At first, it was like a cold that wouldn't go away. I began to become more fatigued than normal. I shook it off and kept going. As my symptoms worsened, I began going to doctors through my completely ineffective HMO plan. Everybody told me there was nothing wrong. After about 6 months of this, my body collapsed. I couldn't get out of bed. I felt like I had mono and the flu at the same time. My ability to concentrate and remember things worsened dramatically.

After a few weeks, I returned to work, only to collapse again a few weeks later. I was permanently let go from Nestlé. Still, no doctor could find anything wrong with me. I started to question my sanity. I actually began praying that they would find cancer or a disease that could be treated rather than endure the limbo of torturous uncertainty.

Finally, I met with a specialist who determined that I had Chronic Fatigue Immune Deficiency Syndrome (CFIDS) and I began the slow road to recovery. For the next six months, I slept an average of 20 hours a day and was able to get out of bed only long enough for a meal and maybe a short walk. It was extremely frustrating to have the desire and motivation to do so much while trapped in a body that wouldn't respond. I didn't share how ill I was with anyone because I didn't want pity or to appear weak. I became somewhat of a hermit. I was able to build up enough stamina to swim 20 minutes a day and had enough energy to work part-time for the next year or so. When I recovered enough to go back to living a "regular life," I found that I had changed.

Finding Life's Passion

Looking back on that painful time, I realize that it was a blessing. Although by all appearances I had seemed successful and happy, deep down inside I was dissatisfied. I was a workaholic; my solution to creating more joy was to work harder. I had no higher purpose to live for and I couldn't see a way out. It was inconceivable to me to quit the job for which I had worked so hard or to rest and let my momentum drop. I couldn't logically find a way out of the trap that I had built, so my body found a way for me.

I believe that, subconsciously, my body collapsed so that I would learn the lesson of balance. I also learned how to follow my heart. Ten years later, when I feel tired or stressed, I realize my body is telling me to take care of myself. I was responsible for my collapse. I see the blessing of that situation; it was a major step on my road to recovery. Appreciating the beauty of each day and the fact that I could move at all enabled me to maintain the positive attitude that was instrumental in my gradual climb to health. I also discovered the need to follow my passions for what I desired instead of what society told me I should do.

Since my recovery, I have started many successful companies, completed my MBA at the University of North Carolina, traveled to 38 countries around the world, and made a profound impact on the lives of many others. I have learned to open my heart, feel life fully, and live each day with passion and connection to other people. I now take care of my body, this extraordinary vessel, by eating healthful foods, exercising regularly, and listening to it when it needs rest or relaxation. I have no desire to return to corporate America. Although many people do not understand my lifestyle, it is the lifestyle that works for me.

My illness taught me many other lessons. When facing a difficult challenge, I allow myself to take one moment at a time. Thinking about how my illness could impact my life and whether I would ever be able to have a normal life again almost overwhelmed me. So I learned to trust the universe/God that it would all work out. I believed that this was all part of a higher plan (which I later learned it was indeed). I learned to focus on the present moment. I also learned to never give up and to overcome any doubts that I would not fully recover. I never really believed that I would stay ill, evidence to the contrary, I also learned that stress is a killer and that crying and laughter are joyous forms of release.

FINDING LIFE'S PASSION

Now I don't stress out about anything. Instead, I revel in the ever changing nature and adventure of life. As I am writing this, I am laughing because I was laid off from my primary job just a few hours ago. Although I loved the company and the work that I was doing there, I am excited about new opportunities that are opening up. I feel no loss or regret and know that something even more profound and magnificent will come my way. I see this layoff as just another step in my journey.

The final, and most important lesson, that makes my life really enjoyable is giving to others. I know that this may sound trite, but it is true. My greatest passion is making profound differences in the lives of others. I am committed to transforming 1 million lives over the next 10 years. Nothing touches my heart more deeply than giving to another. Giving to and loving someone else is also giving to and loving myself. I see now that all human beings are connected. When enough human beings fully understand that harming another is the same as harming oneself and recognize the long-term implications of their actions, peace, joy, and harmony will spread throughout the world as a ubiquitous consciousness.

Scott McClure

GET CLEAR AND FIND YOUR PASSION
Evan Crumpton

I recently heard a story of a young lion cub that had been separated from his mother. As time passed he became very hungry but his mother had not returned. He cried out but there came no response. Once again he cried out in hunger but still there came no response. Finally he let out a bawl in hunger and finally from across the meadow came an answer. The answer did not come from the lion's mother; it came from a sheep that had lost her lamb. The sheep began to nurse the cub and raise him as her own.

The lion began to follow the sheep and learned how to behave like a sheep. When the buffalo herd would thunder by, all the sheep would cower and hide on the side of the meadow and the lion would be right there with them. When the elephants approached the water hole, the sheep would run and hide. The lion would run and hide with them. Every time the sheep were frightened, the lion would also be frightened.

As the lion grew older, it soon became clear that he was different from the sheep. He was bigger than the lambs and they would no longer run and play with him. When he tried to join them, he would knock them down. He began to realize that he was meant to be something else.

One day a mature lion ran to the top of a rock overlooking the meadow and let out a thunderous roar. The sheep cowered, but not the young lion. The mature lion roared again, and deep inside the young lion felt a roar come up through his throat and out of his mouth. He ran up on the rock and took his place next to the mature lion. The young lion had found who he was supposed to be and he claimed his spot.

This story was delivered at a conference by the President of Toastmasters International, Dilip Abayasekara. I am not sure of the origin of the story but it fits my life very well. I spent most of my life trying to please everyone else and forgot about myself. I didn't know how to be myself. I always had dreams but that is all they ever were. I achieved a lot in my life, but I never seemed to really be happy.

FINDING LIFE'S PASSION

I discovered that I had a passion for public speaking and training. I started a business doing that very thing, but spent several years just toying with it. I was allowing a voice in my head to hold me back. It said, "Who do you think you are? What kind of value do you have to offer anybody? You can't do this." I listened to the voice, not even realizing what I was doing to myself. I was that young lion running and cowering with the sheep because I had been looking for my value in other people and listening to negative self-talk. I was allowing other people to determine who I was and what I did.

In January 2005 I attended a conference in Scottsdale, Arizona, called "Maximizing Success." As I listened to the speakers that weekend I began to realize what I had been doing. It was like seeing that old lion roaring from the rock and I realized that what I desired was right in front of me, waiting for me to stand up and claim it. I shed tears many times that weekend, but I left there with a new passion for my life.

I began to claim what was mine and clearly what I really wanted. I have learned since then to look for value in myself and no one else. I realize that I do have value and that I must truly love myself where I am before I can move forward.

I have made many changes in my life since then. In June 2006, I got to share the stage with two of the speakers from the conference in Scottsdale, Steven E. and Gregory Scott Reid. My training business is taking off and I am finally living my passion. Doing what I love and loving what I do.

How do you live a life of passion? Learn to love and value yourself right where you are now. Get a clear vision of what you really want. Look at what you are already passionate about and then ask yourself, "How can my passion bring me what I desire?" The universe will open up a whole new world to you.

Stop running and hiding with the sheep. Climb up on that rock and claim your spot. When you begin to live a life of passion, many new possibilities will open to you. The universe is limitless and so are your possibilities. Claim them now!

Evan Crumpton

THE SECRET PASSION WITHIN
Dorothy J. Walker Wright

The excitement and energy was electric. The conference room was buzzing, the anticipation so intense you wanted to be absorbed. What a contrast to the stale sterile atmosphere of the hotel convention area on the other side of the lobby!

Have you ever walked into a restaurant and felt that same energy and electricity–tables on top of one another, voices vibrating as against a hollow drum, so intensely that you are almost yelling to your companions? Excitement buzzes as the tables are bused quickly and with such expertise, one thinks this art has to be acquired through hours of ambidextrous utility training.

Meanwhile, next door, a restaurant sits empty; highly-polished silver, sparkling crystal, chandelier and proper black tie Maitre'd standing stiffly at the open registrar table.

Why are we drawn to the clutter, clamor, hustle-bustle atmosphere of the cramped tables and boisterous surroundings; the excitement at an intense level? Why do we feel the energy and power in the conference room where 50 women have individual booths, all poised to share their exciting opportunity or new venture they are expanding, with an enthusiasm inexplicably described or demonstrated? Ask a small question and a pouring of enthusiastic replies comes forth with samples and brochures to follow. Where did this electric energy come from?

Why do we want to be a part of this conference or learning center rather than the austere convention center where the presenters are just there to make an appearance with no interaction with the audience?

In the workplace, we have all, at some point, been in a similar atmosphere–cold, calculating, negative energy; a place where no one really wants to be. Compare this to a place of business where things are buzzing. Everyone has a purpose and you can feel the positive energy from the phone receptionist to the forklift driver in the warehouse. Smiles greet new faces and eyes twinkle as if a silent secret resides in each, just waiting to be shared, if only they were asked.

FINDING LIFE'S PASSION

Success versus failure. We ask why does one business, project, or individual succeed and another does not? The road to success is like a journey and each person travels his or her road as a hiker would take to a trail. The hiker must look over the terrain, be aware of the surroundings, have proper clothing to protect against the elements, and make certain food and water supplies are adequate. He or she must have an overall understanding that each path leads to a decision and at some point it may be necessary to change direction to accomplish the climb and reach the expected goal.

It is a secret that we can all tap if we want it badly enough. We all have the ability to capture the great ideas within us and put them to work for us. Each moment in time would be lived in creativity, each hour unfolding unknown truths and new beginnings, living each waking moment in a balance, as nature intended.

We can design our lives–our futures–as an architect builds a structure with a strong foundation, using his design skills and ingenuity. So we build our lives with passion; we create our own reality. Life's passion is lived each day when sharing a bit of knowledge or experience can guide another's destiny in a positive direction.

Whether you have a need to make something better, to share your own special talent, to create or complete that book that will help so many, to start or expand your business that will create jobs and substance with far-reaching positive consequences, or to take a risk, believing in yourself will create your own reality. What a powerful source the human mind is if you follow your passion and live the life you love at the same time. Tap into the energy and excitement inside yourself, discovering the secret passion within you.

Dorothy Walker Wright

FINDING LIFE'S PASSION

CREATING THE FIRE THAT BURNS WITHIN
Matt Morris

After interviewing hundreds of successful entrepreneurs, I've always found one common thread that runs among them: The ability to harness a *white heat of passion* that spills out and envelopes the people around them.

I'm sure you've been around someone like that; someone who just has a special charisma that makes you feel good to be around them and leaves you feeling better about yourself after being in their presence.

That special charisma is what I call their passion! It's an intense emotion that drives them to success; a gut feeling that burns within them and tells their inner being that the goal absolutely *must* be achieved.

I can remember the turning point in my life where I finally "got it." That was the moment I finally made the shift in my life; I no longer would accept mediocrity. I made the real commitment to creating the life of my dreams and living a life filled with *passion*.

We're all either motivated by the avoidance of pain or the desire for pleasure. Unfortunately it took extreme amounts of pain to turn on the lights in my life. It was the time in my life when I hit rock bottom that I finally woke up.

I started a business at 21-years-old. Because of my lack of discipline and lack of vision for my life, I was out of business within nine months. I found myself buried in $20,000 in credit card debt. I was so broke I couldn't afford to make the minimum payments on my credit cards and so broke I couldn't even afford to pay rent.

I took a job as a traveling pool salesman in southern Louisiana in the sweltering heat of July and August. Because I didn't get paid commissions until the pool was actually installed, I ended up living out of my little red Honda Civic five to six nights out of the week parking underneath shade trees so I wouldn't wake up being cooked by the sun.

Because I couldn't afford the luxury of staying in a motel with a shower, I bathed

FINDING LIFE'S PASSION

in gas station bathrooms. One night when I found myself in a city without an open gas station late that night, I actually showered in the rain standing underneath the runoff from the roof of a church.

I remember as if it was yesterday getting back in my car that night and laughing out loud because I thought to myself that I was the absolute definition of *pathetic*. I had truly hit rock bottom. I HAD to find a way to turn my life around. I finally WOKE UP!

That very night I popped in a cassette tape by a man who would soon become my mentor: Tony Robbins. Tony told his story of hitting rock bottom living out of a 400 square foot apartment. (Which actually sounded pretty darn good to me.)

He told his story of going from living a very average existence, to earning over a million dollars a year in personal income. One of the things he had done at an early age was to read over 700 books in the field of personal development. He also talked about modeling other people and that, to be a success, you simply needed to figure out what that successful person did and do the same thing.

I put two and two together and decided that I would, like Tony, start reading everything that would help me train and develop into a success. I started spending every spare moment in bookstores pouring over books on sales, wealth generation, leadership, motivation, communication skills, and anything else that would propel me forward.

I started reading at least one book every 2 or 3 days, and I remember that Tony's book asked you to list everything you wanted in your life and to put a deadline on when you'll achieve it.

That simple exercise of putting *on paper* everything that I could dream was possible for my life opened up a whole new world of *passion*. I quickly learned that dreams are the fuel that fire your passion.

I began visualizing myself having and living everything that I could imagine to be possible for myself. I visualized earning millions of dollars, being able to take exotic vacations around the world, contributing millions of dollars to charity, helping other people become financially free, and being a leader that other leaders would follow.

Now, only 8 years later, I have come to the complete understanding that the more you visualize your dreams, the more you harness your passion. The more passion you live in your life, the more results you create!

I heard a saying many years ago that inspires me to this day and it is something that I would ask you to adopt in your life as well, if you desire to be a leader that others will follow. "Get on fire for your passion and others will come from all over to watch you burn!"

It's that "getting on fire" that's allowed me to go from adversity to prosperity. It's my passion that's allowed me to be the top money earner in sales organizations with thousands of other salespeople, that's allowed me to travel all over the world, that's allowed me to help countless other people earn six-figure incomes, that's allowed me to generate millions of dollars while still in my twenties and to be the CEO and founder of the #1 most popular online personal development learning company in the world, *Success University.*

Because of my *passion* for helping others achieve success, and our team's *passion* for making a difference in the world, we've been able to attract some of the greatest speakers, trainers and authors in the entire personal development industry. We now generate millions of dollars in sales every year, but more importantly, we are helping people all over the world achieve financial and personal success in their lives.

I now wake up every morning completely committed to living every day of my life enjoying and giving to others God's gift of love, happiness and passion!

Figure out what it is that can stir YOUR blood. Discover what it is in you that can create that white heat of passion in your life. Write down on paper everything that you can imagine being possible for your life. Put down everything you could possibly want and then out to the side; put a date that you will achieve it by.

You may not even believe you can achieve it now, but the simple act of putting it on paper will open up the possibilities for you to have them become a reality. I can remember when I created my dream list I had no clue whatsoever as to how I was going to achieve them. Now, just a few years later, I'm astonished at how many of those dreams have actually been realized.

FINDING LIFE'S PASSION

Dream big dreams and use those dreams to fuel your passion. Make a conscious decision to fuel your passion at every possible opportunity and believe wholeheartedly that *your dreams can become a reality*!

Matt Morris

FINDING LIFE'S PASSION

PASSION FOR YOUR PURPOSE... AND THE FREEDOM TO BE WHO YOU ARE
Ilania Heigh Frazier

By design, we are as unique and individual as snowflakes. Even if you are an identical twin there will never be another person who is just like you. Though there are treasure maps hidden in the very structure of your body proclaiming who you are and how you will experience your world, you must have the courage to follow the wisdom that has been handed down from antiquity. This message was so important that the ancient Greek aphorism *"gnothi seauton"* (**know thyself**) was inscribed in golden letters at the lintel of the entrance to the temple of Apollo at Delphi. You must know who you are, how you think, why you react, and what motivates you before you can begin to know others.

Many of us have said, "Oh, I know who I am." Yet, do you truly know how you affect those with whom you are in relationships? Do you know how they really see you? A mirror is biased because only you are analyzing the reflection. We can never see ourselves as others see us. Have you ever had the experience of being with people and feeling uncomfortable? Does your fear of what the world may think or say about you hold you back? Or perhaps you've taken a different approach by saying, "Who cares what anyone thinks!" You barrel ahead, yet find yourself feeling alone even when you are with others. Do you feel love coming to you every day in every way? Are you happy and healthy? Is your life abundant?

You may be bound by the pain of past trauma or broken trust. To say you forgive them and then hold a grudge doesn't work. Over time it will make you ill. To truly forgive is to be set free from all emotion binding you to a situation. Forgiveness gives you freedom from the need to revisit trauma over and over. True forgiveness allows access to the full flow of energy that is yours by Divine right, while giving you the strength, courage, and passion to find and live your purpose with fullness of being.

An analogy I use to describe passion is the wind. Imagine yourself on a sailboat, far from land. The sky is clear and a gentle breeze fills the sail as you glide along without a care. Suddenly the breeze dies down and there is a stillness in the air as the warm sun reflects from the mirrored surface of the water. All is peaceful and calm, yet there is a feeling of pressure. As you scan the horizon the sky is turning dark. The clouds are moving quickly in your direction and the waves begin lapping at the sides of the boat as the wind velocity increases. At this point it is extremely important to be able to harness that wind and direct your boat back to a safe harbor or your very life might be at risk.

Passion, like wind in the sails, requires knowledge and skill. Passion is the ignition key to unlimited possibilities. However, passion without purpose, may take you places you really do not want to go. Very much like the wind, when unbridled passion rages out of control, it can cause extensive damage to self and others. Yet when bridled with purpose, it can make what once seemed impossible an everyday occurrence. To harness the wind you must know when and how to turn the rudder to keep the sail full, or you will be adrift and unable to reach your goal of safety. In life you need a rudder and the knowledge of how to use it properly; otherwise the power of passion is lost and goals will not be reached.

I am so truly blessed to be healthy in body, mind, and spirit with a strong connection to God as my source. One of the greatest gifts I have ever received is finding my passion and discovering my purpose: *"To be the difference that makes a difference!"*

Ilania Heigh Frazier

BE Success - Finding Your Life's Passion
Neil O. Pflum

You are responsible for your life. You are responsible for all of the people, places, and things that currently exist in it. Since you are responsible for your life, you can choose what it will look like. Think of your life as a play; you get to choose whether it is a drama, a comedy, a tragedy, or a farce. You get to choose the actors, the set, and the lighting. It is all up to you. Now that's phenomenal news! So, what will you choose and how will you choose it?

Maybe you will choose to be a millionaire and live a jet-set life. Perhaps you will choose to live modestly in the wilds of the Amazon. Will you choose to spend your life with other people, or will you choose to be alone? How will you spend your time? Will you focus on helping others, or will your concern be more for yourself?

As you can imagine, there is only one person who can answer these questions; however, there are some guiding principles that can help you on your way. Be open to the possibility that each of us is here for a reason. Allow for the possibility that you are part of a master plan, which is not complete without your choosing to be who and what you came here to be.

The part that each of us has to play in the master plan is what I call our purpose or our passion in life. I believe that on some level each of us has chosen this purpose or passion, and that our job here on Earth is to fulfill it. As each of us chooses to live our life's passion, we not only complete our part of the master plan, but we also experience the joy and fulfillment of knowing that we are here on purpose. We have the deep-down satisfaction and peace of knowing that we are unfolding into the flower that is in our nature to become.

Let's assume that you agree and that you would like to find your life's passion, but you aren't sure how to do that. Where would you start? Maybe you aren't even sure that you have a passion in life, but you are open to the possibility. What would be your first step in the exploration process? Start with a look back at your life. Write a history of you. Take your time, and fill in the details. I'm not talking about writing your memoirs over the course of ten years, I'm talking about developing maybe ten pages that chronicle your life. Take a few weeks to write it, then note the significant events. Be willing to feel the feelings that come up as you re-experience your childhood, your teenage years, and your young adulthood. When you have processed what you need to process, go back and look again.

What you may find are events and activities that have a common theme or that actually repeat themselves. Note the ones that have brought you joy. Which ones cause you to lose track of time when you engage in them? These events and activities point to your passion. For example, if you find that every weekend is spent in your workshop making candles, or working with wood, take a closer look. You may find that you spend most of your free time camping in the woods or boating out at the lake. Maybe you find yourself, working with senior citizens or disadvantaged children.

When I look back at my history, I remember my fourth-grade music teacher telling me that I had a lot of talent as a singer, and she asked me to sing a solo in class. I also remember changing the lyrics of popular songs to make fun of my teachers when I was growing up. Now one of my passions is rewriting song lyrics and singing them as part of motivational programs that I present.

If you find that your history doesn't give you a clear direction, check in with yourself. Do some journaling. Spend some time alone, so that you can really consider this question of finding your life's passion. Consider these three most important questions and write your answers:

What brings you joy?

What would you gladly do for free?

What activities, when you engage in them, cause you to lose track of time?

If you already have an idea of what your passion might be, you can "road test" it by taking a small step toward it and watching what happens. For example, if you believe that your passion is to write a book, write a short story or article and submit it to an article submission site on the internet. You can then track the results and see how many people picked up your article. If you are passionate about art, begin a creative project and see how it turns out. Ask some friends for their honest opinion and then ask an artist or two to give you some feedback. You may not be told what you want to hear, but honest feedback is the greatest gift you can receive when trying to discover your passion.

I started out singing karaoke in clubs around Dallas. Then, when I received compliments on my singing, I kept raising the bar little by little, until I was actually getting paid to sing. I sang at nursing homes and retirement homes, then at weddings and corporate events. When I won my first karaoke contest, I held the $100 prize money in my hand and paused on-stage to drink it all in. I could feel, in that moment, that there was more to singing for me than just karaoke.

However you choose to find your passion and live it; just do it! Life is short and should not be wasted. You deserve to have the life you love. Remember, the Universe is not complete without you and your contribution. You need to step up to the plate and live your passion.

Neil O. Pflum

WHAT IS MY LIFE PASSION?
Patrick J. Kiggins

The question should be, "What are my life passions." I grew up as an Army "brat" and have lived all over the world. I found a new passion, every place I lived–swimming, diving, skiing, baseball, football, sailing, rock and roll, golf, auto mechanics, meeting new people, learning about new places, experiencing new cultures, building successful businesses, and the list goes on. I'm also a Vietnam Veteran with several Purple Hearts. I guess you could say that one of my passions is Patriotism. I think the legacy of my parents will be that they instilled in me a dedication to our country and all that it represents. For that, I will be forever grateful.

Over the years, I've become a very confident person and I've learned to think "outside the box," as they say. I'm what many people call a "Visionary." I can imagine how a successful business could be and put plans in place to make that "vision" become a reality.

I learned that skill early in my career at Ford Motor Credit Company. The person who hired me ultimately became the Chairman of that company. My original job was to evaluate the credit risk of commercial loan proposals that were submitted to the headquarters where I worked. Most of the people submitting the proposals were much more experienced than I was.

One day, I was telling my boss that I disagreed with a proposal submitted by one of our most experienced District Managers. I was agonizing over my "assessment" of the situation and told him that I was afraid that there was something in the proposal that I just "wasn't getting" because the person recommending it had so much more experienced than I. That day, I received a speech that I have never forgotten. My boss told me that there wasn't a decision that I could make that would ever send Ford into bankruptcy. And even if (heaven forbid) my decisions ever came close to making that happen, there were more resources in the company that could "fix" my decision before that would ever become a reality. He told me that my job was to make decisions based on my skills, knowledge, and talent. That's why Ford had hired me. After that "speech," I never worried about making a business decision again. In fact, I have used that speech many times over the years to help my employees come to grips with their own feelings of inadequacy.

FINDING LIFE'S PASSION

After working for many large companies and making many "managed, informed risk" decisions, I became a small business owner! I realized that my mentor's words didn't apply to a small business, but I never lost confidence. Ultimately, I was able to start a successful technology company that generated over $5 million in the first nine months of business. I could never have done that without talented employees who shared my vision for the future. Because teaching is another one of my passions, I have always tried to teach my employees how to become successful themselves.

Now I will tell you about my current passion. It might become a passion of yours when you learn more about it. I help Veterans learn how to use their Veteran benefits to start businesses selling products and services to the government. You see, not many Veterans know that our government targets 3% of their contracting budget to be spent with Veterans who start their own business. Now 3% doesn't sound like a big number but it's actually worth about $9 billion a year! The Fortune 1000 companies also are encouraged to spend 3% of their government revenues with Veteran-owned businesses. That adds another $75 billion! All together, our government wants to spend $84 Billion with our Veterans every year.

One problem is that there just aren't that many Veterans who own a business that is qualified to do business with the government. I intend to change that. I let others worry about teaching our Veterans about their medical benefits, their educational benefits and all the other benefits they have. I want our Veterans to know that our government wants to "repay" them for their service to our country. I get e-mails from Veterans telling me their personal stories and phone calls from widows of Veterans asking me for advice. I get joint venture proposals from Veterans who have ideas that could help our government. I also get mail from parents of Veterans who want more information for their children. The response has been overwhelming.

I have created a free newsletter for Veterans. They can sign up to receive it at http://www.veteranbusinessnews.com. I have also written a book, The Veteran Advantage, to teach them every step in the process. I also encourage other businesses to give discounts to our Veterans. What I've experienced as a result of this particular passion is beyond my expectations.

I love working with Veterans in business. They, too, have confidence. They know what it's like to be in a battle where the stakes are so much higher than bankruptcy. I believe that our Veterans (when given the right kind of mentorship) can actually create some of the most profitable businesses we've ever experienced in our nation. I'm committed to making them successful. I invite anyone who wants to help to contact me.

That is my passion and I love it!

Patrick J. Kiggins

EMBRACE SILENCE
Dr. Wayne Dyer

You live in a noisy world, constantly bombarded with loud music, sirens, construction equipment, jet airplanes, rumbling trucks, leaf blowers, lawn mowers and tree cutters. These manmade, unnatural sounds invade your sense and keep silence at bay.

In fact, you've been raised in a culture that not only eschews silence, but is terrified of it. The car radio must always be on, and any pause in conversation is a moment of embarrassment that most people quickly fill with chatter. For many, being alone in silence is pure torture.

The famous scientist Blaise Pascal observed, "All man's miseries derive from not being able to sit quietly in a room alone."

With practice, you can become aware that there's a momentary silence in the space between your thoughts. In this silent space, you'll find the peace that you crave in your daily life. You'll never know that peace if you have no spaces between your thoughts.

The average person is said to have 60,000 separate thoughts daily. With so many thoughts, there are almost no gaps. If you could reduce that number by half, you would open up an entire world of possibilities for yourself. For it is when you merge in the silence, and become one with it, that you reconnect to your source and know the peacefulness that some call God. It is stated beautifully in Psalms, "Be still and know that I am God." The key words are "still" and "know."

"Still" actually means "silence." Mother Teresa described the silence and its relationship to God by saying, "God is the friend of Silence. See how nature (trees, grass) grows in silence; see the stars, the moon and the sun–how they move in silence. We need silence to be able to touch souls." This includes your soul.

It's really the space between the notes that makes the music you enjoy so much. Without the spaces, all you would have is one continuous, noisy note. Everything that's created comes out of silence. Your thoughts emerge from the nothingness of silence. Your words come out of this void. Your very essence emerged from emptiness.

All creativity requires some stillness. Your sense of inner peace depends on spending some of your life energy in silence to recharge your batteries, remove tension and anxiety, thus reacquainting you with the joy of knowing God and feeling closer to all of humanity. Silence reduces fatigue and allows you to experience your own creative juices.

The second word in the Old Testament observation, "know," refers to making your personal and conscious contact with God. To know God is to banish doubt and become independent of others' definitions and descriptions of God. Instead, you have your own personal knowing. And, as Meville reminded us so poignantly, "God's one and only voice is silence."

Dr. Wayne Dyer

Effortless Living Through Magic Mindesign
Michelle Humphrey

Is a great life an accident or is it the result of a magic design?

Do you know anyone who feels good all the time? Who really loves their life? Who has all the money they need to do whatever they wish? Who has great relationships full of love, that bring out the best in each partner? Who has outstanding health with unstoppable energy? Who, no matter what is going on around them, has an attitude that shouts: "Hey! No problem! Got it handled!" Who never complains, gossips or has "a bad day?"

Does that sound like a fairy tale? Does it sound like magic? I thought so too, but such people exist, and I have become one of them. I have discovered three truths that, if believed and incorporated into daily life, can make anyone more productive and positive.

The better you feel, the better your life works.

Nothing can be gained or created if you are feeling turmoil.

There is an effortless solution to any "apparent "problem or challenge.

I am not trying to sugarcoat things and say that a great life is only about positive affirmations, or if you just "let it go" it will all be fine. Living a great life requires applying real skill and having a commitment to live a certain lifestyle. You must begin to believe these truths beyond doubt; that is the point where manifestation occurs.

If you decide to take this journey, it will produce immediate results. Here are some guidelines to help you follow the three truths and get the magic started for you.

1. The better you feel the better your life works

All you have to do is to follow the Law of Attraction: "Like Attracts Like." Common sense will tell you that this is true, but many people fail to utilize it.

Start by writing a list of 100 things you love to do and find ways to implement them in your life. You may have a hard time coming up with 100, but as you begin doing this, your list will grow and you will start to feel better. You will be happier and kinder and you will attract other happy, kind people into your life. Focus your mind on good things; when bad thoughts creep in (and they will) force them out and focus on good thoughts.

Remember: "What is great is what you want to create." You will have to work at it, at first, but eventually it will become habit. Then, you will see the positive results.

2. Nothing can be gained or created if you are feeling turmoil.

There is nothing to be gained by thinking about what you do not like, or complaining about what is "wrong." Stop thinking that you need to "work" on a problem.

But then you ask, "What about the lack of money and my poor health and my nagging spouse; I can't just ignore that!" That is when you must realize that all those negative things are a manifestation of your regrets about your past or your worry about the future. These negative elements rob you of a perfect present moment. Regardless of what is going on, stop giving it a meaning that is not serving you. The answer is to experience the present, and to use all of your senses in doing so.

We only can represent the world – interpret it – with our five senses (That which we see, hear, feel, taste and smell). Regardless of what is going on, stop thinking about it; stop giving it a meaning that is not serving you. Stop and really experience it. Look at what is in front of you, as if it is the first time that you ever saw it. See all the colors, shapes, dimensions, and textures. Then close your eyes and hear everything that you can hear: tones, tempo, distance and direction. Then feel what you can feel: is it hard or soft? Cold or hot? Smooth or rough? You may even taste and smell it.

When you live each moment as a brand new one, no pain can exist. Eventually, you will be able to instantaneously "shift out of" feeling bad.

3. There is an effortless solution to any "apparent "problem or challenge.

FINDING LIFE'S PASSION

Labeling something as "a problem" is part of what makes it a problem. I have since learned to realize that everything is here to bless me. I am excited regardless of what is happening, because I live each moment in a feel-good place; a higher level of consciousness, I can see things from a better point of view. From there, a feel-good place, a win/win, effortless solution, always presents itself.

When something negative shows up, if I resist it and fight it, it will persist and become stronger. If I ignore it or deny it, it won't go away. The real answer is shift your energy and focus on getting to a feel-good place, letting the desired outcome become a reality. The better you feel, and the more you train your mind to only focus on what you want, the easier it becomes to lock your mind on to your desired outcomes.

So if the "problem" is lack of money, shift your energy into first feeling that you are extremely prosperous; picture yourself having the money for all that you desire. See it as if it has already happened. Make it real in your mind by wrapping all of your senses around having it. See, hear, feel, taste and smell yourself living the life that you desire now, with your entire mind and you will start moving toward that reality.

People ask how can I believe in what has not yet happened. The answer is: Faith, the belief in the unseen. You have the power to create all you desire with your thoughts. Your power is in the present moment. Learn to direct your senses and use your mind in a way that will serve you. Start with these three beliefs.

That is what I did. Now my life is not just better, it is truly magical. All of my decisions come from doing the things that light me up and expand my energy. Nothing scares me or makes me mad, because there is always an effortless solution. When you live by these "mile markers" on your journey, you will see desired results manifesting all around you. You will start to see the magic in life.

So the question for you to ask yourself is this: Does a great life happen by accident or by a magic design?

Michelle Humphrey

OBSESSION
Susan H. Paige

I have always been an obsessed soul. My obsessions became my dreams, which became my life. I live my passions. I am married to my best friend and have a career as a teacher, healer, speaker, writer, intuitive and artist. I know I am living my obsessions, because while I am in the act of doing them, like healing or teaching, I feel in a zone. The zone, for me, is a feeling of being in the flow.

But my life was once different. I overcame challenges in my life to get here. Even when I think I have overcome a trauma or challenge, more layers appear within me to look at, work through and overcome in order to create the joy when I am living my dreams in the zone. Being in the zone helps me handle the challenges in life more easily.

My life continues to be filled with many opportunities which I have seized, giving me the personal growth, skills and knowledge to achieve my dreams. It took me 50 years, and just about as many careers and jobs, to be living my passion today.

Even as a kid, I felt I had healing and intuitive abilities. In order to be accepted, I led a conservative life with my job choices: management, sales, marketing and real estate.

Fortunately, I did have a few wise elders in my life who supported my creative side. In my teens, I began my path as a healer. I expanded my knowledge by studying Buddhism, Hinduism, meditation, yoga, healing techniques and natural health. Despite my studies, I stayed in mainstream careers. I had the desire to be a healer, but the comfort level with mainstream jobs was easy and familiar.

At 35, I opened a real estate office in the Chicago area. The stress of the first two years of my business exhausted my body and mind. It was what I needed to make the commitment to be a healer and teacher. I found a two-year certification program that gave me the skills to conduct workshops in personal and spiritual growth. I also took courses in the Reiki, a gentle hands on healing touch. During the time I had my real estate office, I did 24/7 weeks fueled by my passions. At home, I was healer and teacher taking clients and giving workshops. At the office, I was owner and manager, boosting my staff's morale and helping buyers find their dream home. The "at home Susan" helped the "at office Susan."

This lifestyle continued for seven years until my husband came into my life and rushed me off to a new city where, upon allowing the universe to take the lead, I found my dream position. All the parts of Susan could merge as a manger of a large holistic center. This lasted for two years of bliss, until we were transferred to yet another new city.

This proved to be the biggest challenge of all for us both. We missed everyone and everything. I fell back to taking conservative jobs, finding it difficult to find like-minded people. A year later, my husband was diagnosed with Leukemia. I clung to my conservative jobs out of financial fear, but still managed to give some of my workshops around town. After four months of chemo, and many months dreading the future for him, we decided to get off the roller coaster of fear and eminence, and treat his disease as just a part of our lives and not the end of it.

Releasing the fear made room for positive things to appear in our lives. I moved forward with my passion and attended massage school. In the three years since my husband has been in remission, I have created my dreams into my life. I completed massage school and have an active healing practice, managed two wellness centers, given many workshops, and teach Reiki and other courses at a massage school. Together we built a beautiful peaceful new home. My deepest dream had been to have a separate healing room as part of my home, which I now have. I ask every day to be a conduit of love and compassion to myself first, so that I can be a conduit of love and compassion to my clients, all with whom I come in contact. When I allow this, my life is filled with opportunities.

Susan H. Paige

CRYING MAKES ME HAPPY!
Dianea Kohl

My greatest fear was feeling and crying, especially in front of others. Even though my mother cried in front of us, there was always an air of shame around this natural response to hurt. It was like honey hidden in a comb, no taste, only feeling the dislike of its stickiness.

Tears stuck on my blue irises as I stood face-to-face with my tenth grade math teacher to explain that I thought he had incorrectly marked one of my answers wrong. Other students stood waiting as I felt the hot sting in my eyes, fighting not to expose my tears. The memory is as vivid as the pain I stored inside. Over and over again I hid my tears. I was afraid to be criticized for my vulnerability. My human heart.

I saw my grandmother cry only once, tears slowly making their groove down her cheek as she looked at photos of her eldest son, years after he had died in a hit-and-run accident at the age of 21. I was silent. I had no idea what to say. No idea what to do.

I never saw my father cry—maybe tears welled up once as he said goodbye to me when I left for college. In the past decade, I've allowed myself to feel many tears over missing opportunities to cry with him, to share all of ourselves. I love him more so now.

Just last night, I watched the video, Bounce, and was aghast when the adult daughter told her mother not to cry, when they learned of the death of her husband. Can this fear still exist in this new millennium?

My granddaughter, Denali, and I share tears whenever they arise, and they have connected us like stars with the moon. When she was six, visiting her other grandmother in California, she called me in New York, asking me to talk to her grandma Ruth. "Tell her it's okay that I cry, and that I don't have to go to my room. That it's no big deal!" I was so surprised; I jumped for joy! Denali actually had to call her mom in Baltimore in order to find my phone number.

Yes, out of the mouth of babes comes the truth–a truth I model for my family since my heart cracked open during my fourth marriage. I have two daughters from my first marriage to Chuck, which ended when he could admit his gayness, denied by our strict religious upbringing as "born again" Christians. My second marriage to Reid ended when I was able to hear my own heart, the doubt since age 10 that my religious upbringing was not the one-way to God, and I flew free. A few years after our friendly divorce, he learned he had cancer, and died at the young age of 44.

My third marriage, to Alain, came after living with him for a year, believing he had changed, stopped smoking and reduced his drinking. After six months of marital therapy, he didn't want to change, and I needed the intimacy of shared feelings. Marriage number four to Gregory careened me into feelings I had not known existed within me, pain I had covered up with religious brainwashing. Since I was a toddler in weekly Sunday school, I had heard that I was born in sin, unworthy of God's love. I have cried many, many tears over that retrieved memory of emotional pain that nearly crushed my innocent child's loving spirit.

Thankfully, I have awakened from that denial by allowing God-given tears, our body's natural process for sharing our hearts and healing. Since then, I have allowed my rage to be a surfboard. Innocent tears that have washed away my anger and brought true compassion for others. My judgementalness has turned into love of a deeper order. But now my fear of being true in my heart and the fear of being "real" in my life are subsiding. And as a therapist working with and healing others, my mission is to pass this on to everyone. I live to unshamed tears, as Rumi, a 13th century poet said, "When the shell of my heart breaks open, tears shall pour forth and they shall be called the pearls of god." May we all find that freedom, those "pearls of god," that vulnerability that heals our heart.

Never fear tears; never fear your feelings. Revel in life–a gift so great that it must make you cry.

Dianea Kohl

WAKE UP AND LIVE THE LIFE YOU LOVE WITH PASSION
Emmett Sylvester

Greetings: I am Emmett Sylvester and I am excited to share my journey of 66 years with you. It took me a long time to wake up and live the Life I Love. Now, I look forward to each day because I know it will be better than the previous day. I live with passion and know I control my life. I didn't always know how to, so life has been a long journey of trial and error for me. I wish to share that journey with you in the hopes you will Wake up and live the life you love and maybe take a few short cuts along the way.

I was born, like everyone else, innocent and free and, like everyone else, I was influenced by my environment. My mom raised me with love and told me I could do anything I set my mind. My biological father left when I was an infant. I tried to contact him for closure but he did not want to be part of my life. So, my step-father raised me with unconditional love and gave me his family values.

When I was growing up, sports were a passion. I was really good until game time, when negative self talk kept me from playing up to my ability. The coaches didn't teach me how to use my mind to play as well as I could and I was cut from a lot of the teams. With my dreams crushed I started drinking alcohol and getting into trouble. Alcohol and drugs became a way of life for me. When a judge told me to choose between jail or the Marines, I opted the Marines. They gave me discipline and physical abilities but reinforced I was a loser. After 4 years of mental abuse I became a beach bum in California for a couple of years.

My family was in the horse business, so I became a thoroughbred horse trainer, but because of my problem with alcohol, drugs, and stress I had a mild stroke. As things deteriorated, I even filed bankruptcy. It was then I then decided to take control of my life.

I started listening to a self-hypnosis tape by Dr Milton Erickson. Hypnosis helped me to remove resistance to obtaining my goals until one day I no longer had any desire for addictive behavior. I was free. I started to read and listen to any self-help material I could find by men like James, Anthony Robbins, Wayne Dyer, Brian Tracy, and Larry Garretts. I then wanted to help others to take control of their lives. I believe my purpose in life is to help others, so I became a Certified Hypnotist with the National Guild of Hypnotists. My goal was to be the best I could be with out hurting anyone in the process.

In 2002 I went to Harper College to take psychology. I wanted to find out how people thought and why they acted the way they did. It was then that I learned of unconditional love of self and others, non-judgmental listening, and how to use my mind to get what I wanted. I patterned my life after my professor, Dr. Franknosek, and began helping others make positive changes in their lives. But there was still something missing.

I called a friend of mine who teaches people to know and get what they want. He helped me find my passion as an inspirational coach for adolescents. I became a part time school bus driver to learn about how children thought and acted the way they did. I made a positive impact in their lives by listening non-judgmentally, loving unconditionally, and believing they are important. It also allows me to feel good. My school bus is my laboratory on wheels. Today, I am taking courses in children's psychology to learn more about the children and have studied with the top pediatric hypnotists, Don Mottin and Ernest Telkemeyer.

Knowing what I want and allowing it in has made a positive impact on my life. When I wake up each day I appreciate what I have and I know I am living the life I love. I learn from each moment and replace negative thoughts with positive ones and focus my attention on what I want. I am thankful for my wife, an angel who has loved me unconditionally, and given me support and a wonderful family.

With a purpose driven by a passion to help, all things are possible!

Emmett Sylvester

FROM DARKNESS TO LIGHT
Jack Ross

The roads were very slick as I drove to the office one morning. The road that I traveled had no protection from on-coming traffic except for a small grass median. I was in the left lane, mindful of the road conditions, and traffic was stopped on the other side of the highway. Suddenly, a fully loaded cement truck trying to stop, spun around and slid across the median directly into my path.

I knew I couldn't use my breaks and I could not turn left without crashing into the bumper-to-bumper traffic. I would have to turn right in order to avoid the truck, but an officer was standing on the shoulder of the highway directly in what could have been my escape path. I had a split second to make a decision. Was I going to continue my only way of escape at the expense of the officer's life or was I going to continue straight into the oncoming truck at the expense of my own?

I knew what I had to do. I threw myself right parallel to the dashboard and continued going straight–into the approaching truck. On impact, the truck flipped over and landed on my car, crushing it like a tin can. Had I still been sitting in the driver's seat I would have been cut in half by the steering wheel as it crashed through the bucket seat.

Miraculously, I walked away from the horrible crash. There was an ambulance in the same area due to a previous accident. The accident investigator, the same officer who had been walking on the highway shoulder, rode to the hospital with me in the ambulance. The officer was aware that, had I not gone straight into the path of the truck, he would not have been alive to accompany me to the hospital.

I asked the officer if he normally rode with survivors to the hospital. He told me, "Son, I have been investigating accidents for 25 years and I have never seen or heard of anyone walking away from an accident like you just walked away from." "So why are you here?" I asked. "I don't know how or why you are still alive and I am riding to the hospital with you to see if I can find out," he said.

The following day, the picture of the truck and my car made the front page of the newspaper. I was just grateful to be alive. I gave full credit for my survival to a power higher than myself and wanted to find out who this higher power was and devote my life to serving and understanding the one who saved my life. Understanding or "believing" that there are powerful forces in play beyond our consciousness is one thing, but seeking with all your heart to align yourself with this life-giving force is quite another.

While in the hospital, I had to ask myself, "What is the real purpose of waking up anyway? What are we actually trying to accomplish during our stay on this planet?" So I ask you the same questions.

My wake-up call occurred on that very slippery day many years ago. I have found that the "higher power" is indeed the Creator of the Universe. Having gone through my experience and looking back at what happened in 2001, it seems to me that 9-11 should have been our national wake-up call. Each one of us should seek to know the life-giving force of the universe. Our eternal life is dependent upon that knowledge. Yet very few were awakened by that tragic national event. Perhaps we should wake up to the fact that these are serious times and that serious times call for serious action.

The events of 9-11 were tragic, but that is just a sample of what is coming our way. From what I see happening in the world, we should be getting our priorities in order immediately. You do not know when your last breath will be. It is easy to find out what the first four Commandments say. It is quite another thing to know what they mean. To find out about the Commandments and why we should obey them requires intense personal study. You will not likely find truth by sitting on your tail in a church. It takes great personal effort. If you want to be informed and ready for what lies ahead, truth must be your highest priority.

King David was correctly aligned with this truth when he slew Goliath and saved Israel in the process. He had already spent much of his life praying and worshiping the Creator. He was prepared for action. Study King David and align yourself with the true power that he served. Just because someone says they are serving "God," "Lord," "Allah," "J.C.," "the Great Architect," etc., does not necessarily mean they are serving the One and the only Eternal Creator that King David served. Your eternal life is riding on your correct service. When would be a good time for you to get it right?

Finding Life's Passion

It is interesting that Christians, Jews, and Muslims all claim that Abraham (the Hebrew) is their father, yet none of these religions are worshiping as Abraham did. When you place something between yourself and Eternal, you have raised an idol; which happens to be America's favorite pastime. Is it possible that some religious "leaders" have pulled the wool over our eyes and are in fact distracting us from the truth as it was originally intended? Compared to eternity, our physical life represents but a drop in the ocean. What a tragedy to have been diligent enough to polish your little drop to perfection, and yet, to have still missed the vast ocean of eternal life.

When tragedy struck ancient Israel, they knew it was because they had departed from the way of the Eternal. When they returned (repented), things got better. When they refused to return, things continued to get worse. "To you it was shown that you might know that the Lord, He is God; there is no other besides Him," Deuteronomy 4:35.

Not only do we have a responsibility to ourselves to choose Eternal and His way, we have a responsibility to those around us who we influence. Perhaps you are their only source who knows Eternal. It is important for each of us be informed and be available to those who are searching for answers. Will you rise to the call and seek the truth? Will you seek the Creator with all your heart, soul, mind, and strength? Do you know who the Creator looks for on earth? It is those who love Him and obey Him. Are you ready for the challenge?

Jack Ross

The Essence of Leadership
Okneco L. McTier

People usually put their faith and trust in the leaders they choose to follow, whether it be a priest, a minister, a CEO, or an elected official. Yet, people fail to realize that they are the leaders in their own lives. Leadership begins with you, your values and your vision for the future. It's important to remember that every organization, service, and product was created by an individual who had an idea and vision that he/she chose to pursue. The desire and determination to bring forth that vision took action and faith.

People often think of themselves as less important than the politicians they elect or CEO's of corporate America. Many people have bought into the belief that their votes and viewpoints don't matter. However, when it comes to your purpose in life and the pursuit of fulfillment, everything should count. Your life cannot change until you acknowledge and understand its purpose. What are the unique talents and gifts that you can bring forth and share with others? What are you really suppose to be pursuing at this moment? How does the vision for your life fit with the belief system and the decisions that you have made? Are you prepared to take control of your life?

As a child I was told that God had a plan for my life. I was destined to succeed in a field I had no interest in. My thought at the time was that the person sharing this information was tuned into the wrong frequency. Several years have passed and now as I reflect upon that conversation; I realize that the person was right all along. To put it bluntly, I was not ready to take ownership of the information, my path, or purpose in life at that time. I was too busy stumbling with the help of my friends and getting advice from people who had no concept of what I was capable of accomplishing because they had no idea what they could accomplish. They lacked a sense of purpose and purpose in their lives.

Leadership is all about you! It's about your ability to envision a more fulfilled and prosperous life with a higher sense of purpose. We all make decisions that affect our lives daily. Yet, most people fail to accept accountability and responsibility for where they end up in life. If life is a stage and we are simply actors, who do we credit for writing the script or deciding what part we play?

Finding Life's Passion

Individuals who are willing to rewrite the script that no longer suits them are the ones who give themselves permission to become who they were created to be. It's not difficult to be ordinary or simply to fade into the woodwork. However, it does take effort and patience to develop the talents and gifts that are innately and uniquely yours. At this moment in time no one else on earth has your abilities, destiny or sense of purpose. The door is open for you to discover your purpose, reach your goals and share your wealth of experiences and resources with others.

As a leader you must be mindful of the fact that your behavior, decisions, communication style and ethics will constantly be observed and challenged by others. Leadership is a living thing; it's not just about position and money. It encompasses your core being and the very values that direct your actions. You must invest in yourself if you are going to live a life that has meaning and value to you. And there is risk involved. You have to be prepared to ask and answer the hard questions. The goal of self-acceptance and the ability to make the necessary changes will take courage. There are no guarantees, refunds, or exchanges. Faith, strength, patience, and the ability to forgive oneself are all that is required to move forward.

One of the first rules of leadership is to know thyself. What are your strengths, fears, values, and expectations of self? How do you handle a crisis? Do you function well under pressure or are your coping skills somewhat lacking? Are you a risk-taker? Leaders understand that fear has no place in their lives or organizations. There is no magic wand to ensure that everything will run smoothly; therefore, mistakes and errors are bound to happen. Trial and error and growing pains play an essential role in the development of one's character.

Integrity is a key component in building one's character. Leadership requires that one exhibits integrity at all times. The ability to constantly re-evaluate one's emotions, behaviors, beliefs, actions and dislikes are all part of the process necessary for self development, especially in leadership. When leaders truly understand their core values, motives, vision and intentions they can fast forward their lives.

Individuals who are willing to become leaders in their own lives are able chart their own course, in addition, to being able to create organizations that are unique. When individuals develop and enhance their leadership style in all its facets they have the ability to make decisions that represent not only their own interests, but also those of the organization and employees. We must understand that sound decisions are not based on one factor, but many. As we try to elevate ourselves to the role of leader we will surely make decisions that touch the lives of others.

It doesn't matter whether your goal is to be the CEO of your own organization or a better parent or spouse. If you have not defined your core values, goals, self-worth and vision for your life, you will always be on a path that is not your own. Are you destined to excel or merely exist? You are the only one who can decide. If you just stand still, you are making the decision to follow by default. You are telling yourself that you are willing to accept whatever society chooses to give you. As leaders we all have the power to take action in order to move ourselves forward.

This truth is this: Leadership is a reflection of our essence, our soul and character. It's about making contributions to those less privileged, loved one and society at large. We should be able to give time, talents, gifts and love freely to one another. The essence of leadership is about being able to embrace yourself and your purpose in life.

Okneco L. McTier

FINDING LIFE'S PASSION

FINDING LIFE'S PASSION

ARE YOU POSSESSED BY A GOD?
Matthias Schmelz

Every blade of grass has its angel that bends over it and whispers, "Grow, grow." "Enthousiazein" is Greek and means "possessed by a god." I strongly believe that the greatness of God is hidden inside of every living being, particularly human beings.

Nature is so full of wonder, wisdom, miracles, and stunning beauty that we look at it with love, respect, and admiration. In the past, humans protected nature only if it was to their benefit. We differentiated between useful, useless, and harmful animals and plants–depending on whether they could be exploited (cows, sheep, chickens, etc.) or whether they "stole" from us (wolves, foxes, eagles, etc.). We protected the useful, ignored the useless and killed the predators. We actually managed to eliminate many species totally and irretrievably.

Today we acknowledge the worth of every animal and plant. We finally recognize the unique value of each species and its right to exist. Even snakes, scorpions, and tarantulas are entitled to live and are protected by law. Nature does not have to perform any more in order to be preserved. It is only recently that we gave up our arrogant belief that we were God's only children and that every other living creature existed in order to serve us.

Eventually, we accept the responsibility for ourselves and for the environment in which we live. We recognize that everything on earth reflects the spirit of superior creation, and we admit that it is not up to us to decide about who may live and who must die. We humbly acknowledge that the planet we live on was not given to us by our parents, but lent to us by our children. Every tree, every leaf, every snail, and every fish represents a unique expression of the miracle called life, and deserves to be appreciated, admired, adored, thanked for and preserved.

If we respect nature, how much more must we respect ourselves? Aren't we nature's most noble, most brilliant and most conscious results? Aren't we the great-grand-children of the homo-sapiens who not only managed to survive in nature, but who started to shape nature according to his needs? We still have his instincts. We still know how to hunt, how to hide and how to fight. Within a couple of minutes of evolutionary history, we turned into masters of our environment. We have been able to change the world more than any other species. Even the mighty dinosaurs disappeared leaving hardly any trace. Did they die out because they were not able to adapt to a changing world?

Humans have the extraordinary ability to adapt to almost any circumstance. We live on mountain tops as well as underneath the sea. We survive in the desert and we build homes out of snow. We eat fish, meat, grains and fruit. We even create new and very different forms of life. Genetic engineering enables us to eliminate inherited defects. Technology can manipulate plants, animals and the human race. We are following fast in the footsteps of our Father. Are we turning into gods?

I believe that we have always been miniature gods–tiny creators, imaginative ants. Deepak Chopra claims that we are thoughts that have learned to create the physical machine. Didn't we always imagine first and then create? Didn't we always believe before we saw?

If God is our Father (or Mother), shouldn't He or She be proud to watch His or Her children succeed? Aren't we proud when our children do what we taught them to do? The Bible says that God created us according to His image.

Eden Phillpotts wrote that the universe is full of magical things, patiently waiting for our wits to grow sharper. I believe that we just have to keep learning and growing to become who we were meant to be.

Matthias Schmetlz

THE GOLDEN HOUR
Brian Tracy

You become what you think about most of the time. And the most important part of each day is what you think about at the beginning of that day.

Start Your Day Right
Take 30 minutes each morning to sit quietly and to reflect on your goals. You'll find when you read the biographies and autobiographies of successful men and women that almost everyone of them began their upward trajectory to success when they begin getting up early in the morning and spending time with themselves.

Feed Your Mind with Positive Ideas
This is called the Golden Hour. The first hour sets the tone for the day. The things that you do in the first hour prepare your mind and set you up for the entire day. During the first thirty to sixty minutes, take time to think and review your plans for the future.

Use Your Quiet Time Effectively
Here are four things that you can do during that quiet time in the morning.

Number one is to review your plans for accomplishing your goals and change your plans if necessary.

Number two is to think of better ways to accomplish your goals. As an exercise, assume that the way you're going about it is totally wrong and imagine going about it totally differently. What would you do different from what you're doing right now?

Number three, reflect on the valuable lessons that you have learned and are learning as you move toward your goals.

Practice Daily Visualization
Number four; calmly visualize your goal as a reality. Close your eyes, relax, smile, and see your goal as though it were already a reality. Rewrite your major goals everyday in the present tense. Rewrite them as though they already existed. Write

FINDING LIFE'S PASSION

"I earn X dollars." "I have a net worth of X." "I weigh a certain number of pounds." This exercise of writing and rewriting your goals everyday is one of the most powerful you will ever learn.

Fasten Your Seatbelt

Your life will start to take off at such a speed that you'll have to put on your seatbelt. Remember, the starting point for achieving financial success is the development of an attitude of unshakable confidence in yourself and in your ability to reach your goals. Everything we've talked about is a way of building up and developing your belief system until you finally reach the point where you are absolutely convinced that nothing can stop you from achieving what you set out to achieve.

Everything Counts

No one starts out with this kind of an attitude, but you can develop it using the law of accumulation. Everything counts. No efforts are ever lost. Every extraordinary accomplishment is in the result of thousands of ordinary accomplishments that no one recognizes or appreciates. The greatest challenge of all is for you to concentrate your thinking single-mindedly on your goal and by the law of attraction, you will, you must inevitably draw into your life the people, circumstances and opportunities you need to achieve your goals.

Become a Living Magnet

Once you've mastered yourself and your thinking, you will become a living magnet for ideas and opportunities to become wealthy. It's worked for me and for every successful person I know. It will work for you if you'll begin today, now, this very minute, to think and talk about your dreams and goals as though they were already a reality. When you change your thinking, you will change your life. You will put yourself firmly on the road to financial independence.

Action Exercises

Now, here are two things you can do every single day to keep your mind focused on your financial goals:

First, get up every morning a little bit earlier and plan your day in advance. Take some time to think about your goals and how you can best achieve them. This sets the tone for the whole day.

Second, reflect on the valuable lessons you are learning each day as you work

FINDING LIFE'S PASSION

toward your goals. Be prepared to correct your course and adjust your actions. Be absolutely convinced that you are moving rapidly toward your goals, no matter what happens temporarily on the outside. Just hang in there!

Brian Tracy

SUGAR, PASSION, AND HAPPINESS
Helen Shanley

As a child, I knew I walked in the sunlight of God's love. I was blessed at an early age.

I recognized all of the colors at six months and talked at eight months. I began walking at ten months and reading at two and a half. My advancement continued; I could say the Latin names of, and point to, the parts of the brain and the bones of the body, and knew the capitals of all 48 states by three and a half. At the age of six, after reading the Old Testament stories and the entire New Testament, I asked to be baptized. I adapted a book into a play, which I directed, starred in, prompted and produced for the school assembly at seven. A semester before, I was doing second-grade level hand work, third-grade level arithmetic, fourth-grade level geography, seventh-grade level spelling, and eighth-grade level reading. No one was pushing my development. I loved my life.

When I turned 14, my world crashed around me. I have spent most of my life trying to put it back together. Along the way I did some writing, earned college degrees, developed a new way of teaching and took ministerial training, but I wasn't happy. I felt I had failed in so many ways. Because of this repeated feeling, I felt doomed to be always on the verge of success, only to fail. Yet, I knew from experience that happiness is the truth of life.

Recently, it occurred to me to ask for fulfillment as a way to overcome these feelings of failure and the sense of guilt that followed. I knew I needed to surrender to this fulfillment.

Now, at age 85, I'm living a life I love. I'm a licensed practitioner of religious science. I do everything I love: singing in the choir; being with people; praying for them and seeing their lives transformed. I teach Sunday school children that they individually can have what they want, and how to help themselves. I use depth imagery in transformational meditation services. I get speakers for my writer's club, facilitating both poetry and fiction groups and I do creative editing. I offered a simple exercise class in my neighborhood, and after 25 years people now greet me by name when I take my walks.

FINDING LIFE'S PASSION

Sugar on My Lettuce, the first book in a three-part memoir, is being published. My stories and poems are broadcast over Valley Public Radio. The poems and stories I'm writing now are among the best I have ever done.

Even though much of this was going on before I asked for fulfillment, I wasn't happy. Now, I know the universe wants me to succeed. I'm not trying to accomplish anything, not pushing a stone up a hill. I'm allowing myself to be fulfilled.

Anyone can do this sort of turn-around. It's definitely worth it. And I'm worth it.

Helen Shanley

FINDING LIFE'S PASSION

"GET UP NOW" – *THE 3 SECRET STEPS TO SUCCESS*
Mark Bradley

L ike many kids, I was a dreamer and I was always "getting into things". Luckily I was born with a great work ethic. At age 13 I was captain of my junior league football team and had worked full time for 3 summers cutting lawns. That thirteenth summer I was really motivated because I wanted a shiny 5-speed Stingray bike. By midsummer I had earned enough money to buy it. It was beautiful, cherry-red metal flake paint, shining chrome fenders, stick shift, and a racing slick rear tire. Things were good! I can still recall that new bike smell.

One afternoon after work, my friends and I rode our bikes to one of our favorite places. There was a huge oak tree with a rope swing. On one of my turns to swing, the rope slipped out of my hands and I fell over 30 feet to a dry creek bed. I remember hearing a voice saying, "Mark, you gotta get up!" My friends put me on my new Stingray and walked me home. The fall caused a concussion and I didn't wake up for two days.

Just a few years later, I had dropped out of high school and my life was going nowhere. But somehow I was able to get up again. My brother John straightened me out and helped me focus and apply for college. I graduated with two degrees. After that, I began to succeed in business and in my personal life. Then the rope slipped from my hands again. One day I came home and my wife had taken my three young children and moved to a city four hours away. Not only that, she had married a friend of mine. At almost the same time I was fired from my job. Needless to say, I was devastated. Once again, I had to "Get up."

From that experience and others from my past I formulated my first secret step to success: When you get knocked down or fall, you must get back up. Don't wallow in misery or self-pity.

When I got up this time, I started my own real estate investment company. I carefully acquired millions of dollars worth of investment properties, developing great relationships with my lenders along the way. Everything I touched seemed to turn to gold. I could not have achieved the success I had if I hadn't gotten back up.

FINDING LIFE'S PASSION

I was about to learn that there are other steps to success that must be applied. It was September 11, 2001. I had invested heavily into two major real estate projects. Everything I owned was on the line. When the Twin Towers came crashing down, so did my finances and my dreams. Once again, I felt as if I was lying on that creek bed. This time, the voice came from within: "Get up."

But how? All I could think about was all the things I had done wrong, all the failures, all the regret. That's when I found the Second Secret Step of Success: You must forgive yourself so you can move on with your life.

When I finally applied Step Two, a whole world of possibilities opened up. My past failures were just learning experiences and resources to be drawn upon. All of the bad was behind me and I could look to a brand new future loaded with promise and possibility.

There was a third step that was needed to complete my turnaround. For me, it was as if I had been driving in a fog for a long time; suddenly, the fog lifted. I saw everything I'd been missing. The Third Secret Step of Success is Refocus. If you don't refocus you won't really know how to do the "moving on" of Step Two. You must find your passion and purpose. Ask yourself, "What has to be true for me to be happy and fulfilled right now? If I was, what kind of person would I be?"

Now, begin to live that life today. Be that person today. Get up now, forgive yourself so you can move on, and then refocus on being the person you want to be. When you follow these three steps, you will move toward success and will be living the life you love.

Mark Bradley

DON'T PLAY IT SAFE
Rina Hafiz

All my life I played it safe. Our family motto was "better safe than sorry." In college I selected "safe" teachers, those in whose class I could get the "A." I got a nice, safe degree in electrical engineering, followed by a safe job with the government, safe relationships and so on. But there was a part of me wanting something more; I didn't know what I wanted, so I had no idea how to get it. I never would have guessed that "playing it safe" was to blame.

When the opportunity for a business in cosmetics came along, something inside of me said, "Yes," without any analysis or thought. For once, I trusted my gut feeling. I didn't even think, "Do I really want to sell lipstick?" I was trying something new, and that longing for having more in my life started to be fulfilled. Naturally, with the new business, I played it "safe," by telling no one what I was doing. I worried about what people would think, and I settled for building with fear.

Even though I had become a success in business, I still refused to let go of a full time engineering position. Engineering was predictable, easy and secure. I convinced myself that it was good to have a safety net. Looking back, I realize now that the net was really over me instead of under me. It was a belief limitation keeping me from soaring higher.

I truly feel blessed for having the opportunity to start a business instead of staying with safe corporate America. Because of an extensive education, personal growth and the new skills I developed in my business, I now live the life I love. Building your own business forces you to face your communication flaws and overcome each one.

My original goal was to make enough to have someone clean my home. My husband felt that having a maid was a waste of money. I vividly remember the first time our house was cleaned. We had a fine crystal chandelier in our dining room that we had bought in Prague; I came home that day to see my husband staring at the chandelier with all the lights on. I asked him what's going on. He said, "Did you know it's not frosted glass?" I looked at the lights and realized the glass wasn't frosted anymore. Since then, I haven't vacuumed in seven years, and the house is always clean.

Finding Life's Passion

Because I stepped out of my comfort zone, we were able to build our dream house on five acres. I have a gourmet kitchen for decoration purposes only because someone cooks for us. We have someone else mow the grass, but we play soccer on it with our kids. In kindergarten, my son had so many airline miles that he was getting credit card offers in the mail. I put my kids on the bus in the morning and I am there when they get off in the afternoon. I go to the school when I want, go on any field trips I want, I'm secretary of the PTA and still make a great income. All I gave up was housework, constantly balancing my check book and living for Fridays. I put away the boring cars and earned a pink Cadillac!

I have always been great at money management. When I first started working as an engineer, I lived off half my salary. The rest I saved or invested. Later on when I got married, I lived off one third of what I made. But even at that savings rate, I would never have achieved what I have today. The reason for this is that, in business I learned how to set goals and reach them, and having only one source of income is so over taxed, it is no way to get ahead. Not only have I invested for college educations for four kids, but we are also giving back to our parents. And regardless of what our children or parents do with our gifts, I have learned not to be attached to the outcome of their decisions. Total freedom is knowing that you control your choices and allowing everyone else to learn from theirs. I am free from what others think, what they will say, or what they might do. I have the luxury to only invest in what I think.

I remember staring at my cubicle walls one day and being so frustrated with my job that I wrote down a description of my perfect life. I wanted to watch the kids play on the swings while I worked on my deck, and worked with only people I liked. After I wrote my description I remember looking out of the window and seeing people in the July heat keeping the lawns on the complex. I thought, "They are so lucky to be outside today." A few years later I read this description. I get to plan every day; I have more time to do what I want; I am the major influence in my kids' lives and can take a vacation anytime I want. Once you decide on the life you want, you have to find the courage to live it.

Rina Hafiz

Finding Life's Passion

Angel
Benson A. Wong

I remember the morning my father woke me up to tell me that my little sister, Jennifer, had passed away. I was stunned by his words because it was totally unexpected. I was eight years old and Jennifer was only seven. We were very close–laughing and playing all the time. I can't even remember a single time we had ever fought.

Following Jennifer's passing, I felt emotionally drained. I tried to understand what death meant. Whenever I thought about Jennifer, I felt so much pain and sadness in my heart because I really missed her physical presence. I spent many nights crying myself to sleep. Finally, one night, there were no more tears.

Shortly after Jennifer's passing, I wanted to see if I could communicate with her. As I lay in bed and gazed out my window at the stars above, I said softly, "Hi Jennifer, I love you." Almost immediately, I felt light-headed as my spirit lit up. I heard Jennifer say, "Hi Benson, I love you too." I reached out with my hand and felt the warmth of her energy. The pain and sadness I had felt in my heart eased and was replaced with exhilaration. From that moment on, I was certain that Jennifer was still around, and I could communicate with her at any time.

I recently realized that Jennifer's passing led to the awakening of my clairvoyant and healing abilities. Whenever I thought of Jennifer with my heart, I felt pain in my chest and stomach. But when I thought of her with my head, it was a different experience. Just as the first time we communicated, I became light-headed, and exhilaration replaced the pain.

With that bit of information, I learned that I could create and have almost anything I wanted, with little effort. I made up a fun game where I would think of something I wanted or someone famous that I wanted to meet, and usually received what I wished for. But, sometimes, when I got too serious and put too much emotion and effort into my wish, it would not come true. So I learned to relax and create in a light, happy space instead of a serious space. I wasn't always consistent in creating this kind of space while growing up. Like most teenagers and young adults, I rushed around and got impatient at times, which affected my ability to create and my level of achievement.

In my early twenties, my interest in learning more about the metaphysical world grew. I met a person named Lee Hinton who became a dear friend and brother. Lee and I have a real spiritual connection. Lee encouraged and motivated me to actively use my clairvoyant abilities. We validated each other.

I started reading various books on metaphysics and attended meditation and healing classes to gain more knowledge. I started doing readings, and soon, friends and co-workers started asking me questions about their love life, relationships, family, health, money, career, clairvoyant abilities, etc. They enjoyed their readings and kept referring others to me.

Many people are curious about how my readings work. The type of reading that I do is called a clairvoyant reading. A simple definition of clairvoyance is the ability to sense mental images, sounds, and different levels of energy that the average person isn't consciously aware of. My readings are conducted in a professional, sensitive, simple, and confidential manner. My objective is to provide a safe, enjoyable, comfortable, and informative experience for my clients.

It is very important to be in a neutral space while performing a clairvoyant reading. One must not become too attached or emotional, because it can affect the quality of the reading. It is important to be able to release the energy of the person after the reading. You must not become affected by their problems/challenges, because your health can be affected.

During readings, as I focus my attention on the person, I receive information about their personality, creative abilities, health, and relationships as well as experiences from their past, present, and future. I receive this information by looking at their "aura" (the energy surrounding the body) and their "chakras" (the energy centers located within the spiritual body).

The readings may include information about how my clients can use their own abilities to balance and heal their spiritual selves and their physical bodies.

I really enjoy doing readings because each one is different. Each person has different information, experiences, challenges, wants, needs, and goals. When a person comes to me for a reading or healing, I get such a tremendous feeling of gratification watching that person transform from feeling depressed to feeling amazed, happy, and on top of the world.

I am often asked how I developed my clairvoyant abilities. I believe it has had a lot to do with my passion for learning and my desire to help others. I keep an open mind and am always observing people. To sharpen my skills, I take long walks with my wife, Cathi. As people pass by us, I quickly read them. Sometimes I read up to several hundred people in our 4-hour walks around San Francisco. If you do something for a long time, you become very good at it. I have performed over 100,000 readings, healings, and workshops in the past 30 years, and have become very good at what I do.

I've developed a seven step program called, "Feel Good Now. Discover the Hidden Messages within You." This program will help you find out who you are as a spirit, what you are holding on to from your past and how it affects you, what lessons you are learning in this life, what you are creating for your future, and much more. The ability to use my clairvoyant abilities to help others find their happiness and spiritual growth is truly a gift from God, and it all began when God brought me that little angel, Jennifer.

Benson A. Wong

THE BEST INVESTMENT YOU CAN MAKE IS IN YOURSELF
Ned & Cheryl Rae

I grew up in the small New England town of Granby, Massachusetts, the kind of town where bad news beats you home at night. I was the middle child in a middle class family with big dreams! In 1968, I was drafted and served honorably in Vietnam.

I was not the same in 1972 when I was discharged. The next decade was a blur of drugs and alcohol. I had two children and a failed marriage. I had been able to hold a machinist job despite my bad habits. Eventually I moved to Dallas, Texas, in 1981, where I met Cheryl. I asked myself, "Who would I have to be to keep a lady like that interested in me?" The answer was clear–the young man my parents had raised me to be. That night I cut all ties to my alcohol and drug past.

Cheryl was raised in Irving, Texas, the oldest of four children in a middle class family. She was told to graduate from high school and go work for a company with good benefits and stay there until she retired. Her first job was as a book-keeper at a bank. She met a loan officer there who kept telling her that with the skills she had, she could be doing much more with her life. We all have cheerleaders in our life–Hank Goldsmith was hers. He referred her to a good friend of his at The Wall Street Journal, where she began her career. By the age of 22 she had been married, divorced, was a single mom, and had lost her daughter, Amii, in an accident. More adversity than most go through in a lifetime.

I met Cheryl and six months later we were married. My parents thanked Cheryl for bringing home the boy they raised. We got custody of my children from my first marriage and they came to live with us in Texas. Tonya was 11 and Jason was 10. After seven years of marriage, Cheryl and I decided to have a child together. Our son, Nathan, was born August 25, 1989.

Cheryl and I both worked in corporate America with very good-paying jobs. I was working 60-70 hours a week, mostly on the evening and night shifts. When Jason crossed the stage at his high school graduation I realized that I had missed his and Tonya's childhoods. I was so busy making a living, I had

Finding Life's Passion

traded my life's hours for dollars. I promised myself I would not miss Nathan's years of growing up.

I was working my usual Saturday shift when a co-worker asked me a question. "If time and money were not an issue in your life, what would you be doing differently?" That was my introduction to Free Enterprise. I went to my first opportunity meeting and I got excited about building a "Plan B" for our future. Cheryl, on the other hand, was not so enthused. She said she would support me and be my cheerleader but not to ask her to sell or talk to anyone. I finally convinced Cheryl to go to our first conference, where she fell in love with the people and the concepts of Free Enterprise. She realized that job security was becoming a thing of the past. We asked ourselves: Where would we be five years from now if we did not do this? Where would we be if we did and it worked? She decided the fear of starting over with another company was greater than the fear of learning this business. We became a team and never looked back.

Then we started down the road of personal development. We began reading books like Think and Grow Rich, How to Win Friends and Influence People, Personality Plus, and The Magic of Thinking Big. We attended every seminar that was promoted to us. We turned our car into a rolling university. We were like sponges–hungry for the information and determined to succeed no matter what it took.

Our first endeavor was a failure, or so we thought. But we knew that even traditional businesses don't expect a profit for five years. Everything was going out and nothing was coming in. I left my job to do Free Enterprise full time, before I really should have. Soon there were debts and a bankruptcy, not to mention foreclosure notices. I read the books, attended the seminars, did everything we were told to do, only to fail and fail again. This is where so many people quit–three feet short of gold. But I was not going to give up. Once your mind expands there's no going back and settling for less. Cheryl's mom suggested that we find someone who had been successful in this business and who was willing to teach us what they did. So, we found a mentor.

In 2001, I answered a newspaper ad that had caught my attention. I met a sharp young man by the name of Matt Morris. I knew this kid was sharp. That young man forever changed my life. His mentorship taught us a system and we began to have success. We had lasted through the learning curve. There's a price to be paid to be successful and a price to pay to stay the same. There will come a time when you're either glad you pursued your dream or wish you had.

Matt's dream was to build a school that teaches entrepreneurship. He called us when he was ready to pre-launch Success University. We came on board and helped him launch that dream on January 24, 2005. As Matt had told me several years before, opportunity seeks out and finds the prepared mind. We are Executive Directors with Success University and earn a five-figure salary every month. Before, our life was lived paycheck to paycheck. We got sick and tired of being sick and tired and decided to take action. Now we make money on multiple time zones. Imagine making money while you're sleeping! I have been a "stay-at-home" Dad for the past six years. We now have the option to live our lives the way we had always dreamed.

Success is a process. It's who we become on the journey. Success and wealth principles do not change. If they work for one, they work for all. We learned these principles and we applied them to our life. The best investment you can make is in yourself. We are passionate about helping people achieve their dreams. Imagine getting up every day and doing what you love to do and making a difference in other people's lives. Our good friend, Gary Eby, says that change is a door that can only be opened from the inside. What changes are you willing to make to Live the Life YOU Love?

Ned & Cheryl Rae

FINDING LIFE'S PASSION

THE $25,000.00 DOLLAR KNOCK
Jeffery Craig Shirley

We have all read, heard or seen on TV how others have taken advantage of opportunity when it knocked. When was the last time opportunity knocked on your door? Think about that for a minute now!

One day, while visiting a friend at home, the doorbell rang; I went to the door. A woman was standing there, and she introduced herself as the fiancé of Jim, the owner of the property next door. She said, "I noticed you had your house up for sale. Did you sell it already?"

"No," I told her, "the owner took the house off the market and plans to sell it at a later date." I continued the conversation by asking her why she was interested.

She replied, "We are interested in selling the property next door when the renters move out at the end of the month, and are looking for a quick sale because the young men living there trashed the place."

"May I ask what are you selling the property for?"

She replied, "One hundred and seventy-five thousand dollars."

I had a good idea of what property sold for in the neighborhood, and I knew this was quite a reduction of the retail price. I said, "Not to offend you, but I will offer $170,000.00 in cash, one week from today, if you sign a contract today!"

She replied, "Let me speak with Jim, and we will let you know tomorrow."

Before she left that evening, we exchanged phone numbers. After speaking with Jim, he assured me I would be hearing from him. The next day I waited patiently. Then, I received a call asking me what would be a good time to come by to sign a contract.

It was a great relief for Jim to be free of the property. He no longer had to be available at all hours of the day to show the property to potential buyers. Jim told me that his father, who lived in California, was the real owner, and he planned to give the money to him. Jim wasn't in a hurry to get the money, even though his tenants were moving out in two weeks and he knew he would have to make the next mortgage payment. He was relieved he wouldn't have to make any payments after that.

After speaking with him for a short time, he agreed to let me go in after the tenants moved out to start my renovation. We had the understanding that if I didn't close by the end of the month, I would make the mortgage payment.

This was really turning into a win-win situation. Thank God for that! I had to make only one mortgage payment before I sold the property for a profit of $25,000. And, I never had the $170,000 to pay cash in seven days. I only had my faith in the means to locate OPM (other people's money).

Looking at a cup of water, I like to see it half-full, as opposed to half-empty. Anyone can see it half-empty. The key is to surround yourself with people who have a positive mental attitude. That attitude alone will give you the energy you need to step out with faith. Now, ask yourself, "How many people do you I know would have answered the door ready to jump on an opportunity?" How would you have answered the door? Would you have been quick to turn her away? Opportunity knocks everyday in so many different ways, whether you're dealing with real estate or not. Are you willing to listen and explore with great boldness when opportunity knocks. Opportunity's knuckles are raw from knocking on your door. Will you take time today and listen?

Jeffery Craig Shirley

Finding Life's Passion

PICASSO OF THE SEA
Wyland

Many years ago, while visiting friends at the Dolphin Research Center in the Florida Keys, the Director, Mandy Rodrigues, asked if I would like to paint with some of the dolphins. Of course, I wondered how this was going to work. I made my way to a lagoon where, to my surprise, a small group of bottlenose dolphins greeted me with excitement.

As I sat on the edge of the dock and readied my water-based acrylic paints, the dolphins became even more excited. I, too, was excited about collaborating with these highly intelligent mammals of the deep. If any animal on earth (besides humans) could create a work of art, it most certainly would be dolphins.

I passed a paintbrush to a dolphin named Kibby, who took the handle in her mouth. Next I held up a canvas and she began immediately to paint in the style of Picasso, laying down each stroke with a twist of her head and, finally, with a 360-degree spin. When she was done she passed the brush back to me and watched as I painted my part.

As two very diverse marine artists, Kibby and I shared a single canvas. But discovered that we also shared something else—tears of joy. Together we had created something uniquely beautiful; a one-of-a-kind collaboration between two artists of two completely different worlds.

Later, I told my friends on the dock that it was just the salt that made my eyes water. But they knew it was the feeling I had for my newfound friend of the sea.

When the painting was finished, Kibby smiled a big dolphin grin. She nodded her head in approval of the completed work, then lifted her flukes above the surface and dived below. A few seconds later she brought me the highest honor a dolphin can give: a gift from the sea. It was a rock!

There are wonders in this world; wonders of which we haven't dreamed. Seek new places; find new friends, and wonder with me.

Wyland

Finding Life's Passion

The Gift of Opportunity
Alice Inoue

It is a gift to have the opportunity to write my story, and I've found when I open myself up to gifts, the opportunities keep coming. It is the opportunities that I've taken that contribute to living a life that I love. It can be the same for you – once you realize the gift of opportunity is there for you to take every single day.

My mother is a beautiful, wise Chinese woman. She grew up in extreme poverty and was 26 years younger than my father. My father was a mean-tempered but good-hearted merchant marine who never finished the sixth grade.

I first learned of seizing opportunity from my mother's story, which I heard many times. Her world was strictly about survival. She would sometimes go days without food. When she met my American father and he declared his love for her, she saw it as a huge opportunity knowing it was her only way out of a desperate life, despite the fact her family threatened to disown her. She saw the gift of opportunity, married my father and came to America.

After I was born, we moved to Taiwan where I soon learned to speak Chinese.

Through the years, the adults would always speak to me about "ji whei," meaning opportunities. "Alice, look for the "ji whei;" don't pass up any "ji whei," and don't hesitate when a "ji whei" presents itself." Following this advice has done so much for me on my journey of life.

What I grew up noticing about the Chinese culture was that once they identify an opportunity, they jump on it without hesitation, knowing that they lose out if they don't. Since Taiwan is so overpopulated, there's much competition. Hesitate, and someone will beat you to it, the way bridesmaids jump for the bride's bouquet at a wedding reception without fear or wavering in their purpose.

I took this advice and this way of looking at opportunity to heart, and it became my way of being as I left Taiwan to attend college in America. It is only now that I can look back over the past 25 years, and realize it is seeing the gift of opportunity that has allowed me to live so happily and so fully.

I have never regretted an opportunity that I have taken. In retrospect, absolutely everything I've done has enhanced my experience of life on multiple levels. Not that it was all easy, but what it really did was open me up to the fullness of what life has to offer.

The universe provides opportunities daily, though it may not necessarily be a gift of money or a gift of being able to write in a book, but the "gift of opportunity." You only have to look to see opportunity in front of you every day of your life. Open yourself up to the journey of the experience, and you'll see all the gifts the universe offers can be claimed as yours.

Alice Inoue

FINDING LIFE'S PASSION

WHO TOLD YOU TO GET COMFORTABLE?
Dr. Stephen Hudson

One of the biggest problems is that life is too easy. You don't have to walk five miles for clean water; you don't need to go hunting to feed you or your family, and you didn't have to build your home with your own two hands. Some people still have to do this but not you. You are lucky with a nice, cushy job, gadgets galore and a nice leather sofa. Life is very comfortable, isn't it?

Herein lies the problem. We spend most of our lives in a "comfort-zone." We say, "I just bought my 42" surround sound TV, now my life will be that much better." Really?

In reality, the comfort zone isn't particularly comfortable and will result in constant challenges such as unexpected bills, poor health, and bland relationships. This is life's way of trying to get you to change because humanity, in its wisdom, likes the comfort zone. Mankind has invented distractions: you have to get that report done by Friday, can't do it tonight–Monday Night Football is on TV, I'll study for my test next week, I'll go to the gym tomorrow, I don't want to miss *The Simpson's.*

Distractions are a big problem. They include:
- TV, DVDs, videos, computer games, and Internet
- Alcohol
- Non-nutritious food
- Sports
- Gossip
- Holidays
- Gadgets and "must have items"
- Pornography
- Drugs – legal and illegal
- Sex
- Newspapers/magazines
- Trashy novels

I sound like a right-wing moralist, don't I? Well, as it happens, I am wearing my moral jackboots as I write this. Some of the distractions can be used to empower your life. The Internet can be an amazing source for research; sex is great, period, and holidays are part of enjoying life. They are called distractions because the vast majority of people engage in them to an excess. Instead of deferring their pleasure, looking after their bodies and making enough money so that they can live the life of their dreams, they get caught up in excuses and distractions. The result is they end up living a mediocre life. Reject that half life; get passionate!

Assuming you want to change your life, is watching ER going to give you a better life? Wouldn't studying for that class get you to where you want to go a little quicker? You decide, because when you combine distractions with excuses, then we have the current comfort zone for most of the western population.

Now, no one is suggesting that you should remove all of life's pleasures. But you should not indulge in them when there are more beneficial things to do. You should not live your life for your pleasures. Pleasures should be your rewards. Don't live for the comfort zone. The problem is, in the long run, the comfort zone is far from comfortable. It is an illusion. Why? Life is a harsh mistress. She demands the best from her children, and if they don't live up to her expectations, she will make them suffer. The suffering is designed to get them to change their ways. This is, in the long run, for our own well being. Most of the time, we don't listen, and when we don't listen, we suffer.

Dr. Stephen Hudson

ALLOW YOUR PURPOSE TO SURFACE
Ann M. Preston

"What do you want to be when you grow up?" Ask this question to any child and they will say things like become an astronaut, a movie star or a famous ball player!

Where is that dream now? Just because you may be in your 40s and you sell "widgets" doesn't mean your dream is not somewhere deep inside of you. I believe everyone has a purpose. They just need to allow it to surface.

Several years ago I lost someone I loved very much. She was like a daughter to me and I was devastated. While I was deciding what to do next, I picked up Deepak Chopra's book, *The Seven Spiritual Laws of Success*. While reading his book, I got the idea that would change my life. I found my purpose. It was within me all along!

You see, life has a way of beating us down and forcing us to conform to ordinary roles. It's just like the story about the goldfish. He can only grow to a certain size, depending upon the size of his fishbowl. Move him to a beautiful outdoor pond, however, and he can grow one hundred times the size.

I had been a shy, scared, tiny goldfish living inside my tiny, little fishbowl. When I allowed my purpose to surface, I rediscovered my childhood passion for being a leader among the other kids, for directing and putting on shows in our basement and for never losing a race–even against a boy.

Now, I am a successful entrepreneur who teaches others how to realize their dreams and succeed through the system I created the day I found my purpose.

I am a leader of thousands of business people. I produce life-altering shows with world-class speakers, and whenever I have a challenge in my business or in my personal life, I never lose a race! My greatest passion is to help others succeed. My purpose and my organization, Freedom Builders, provides a forum for others to build their business and stretch their vision every day. My dream has grown from creating the best business success system ever created, to completely revolutionizing

FINDING LIFE'S PASSION

the sales process worldwide, by spreading Freedom Builders concept of *The New Way to Sell* across the globe!

I couldn't have created such a massive system without "the other kids on the block." Once you've allowed your purpose to surface, you need to share it with others. People are our greatest gifts. Don't be afraid to share your dream because, when you do, the person sitting next to you could be the one to make that dream come true.

Create a Team & Realize Your Dream.

> Together vs. apart (in mind, spirit and outcome)
> Everyone participates fully
> Admit your shortcomings
> Make each other's dreams come true
> Willing to do for others as much as for yourself
> Overcome hurdles together
> Recognize, reward and restore each other
> Keep sharing this concept until there's no one left to share it with

So don't wait until life stops you to find your purpose. Take the day off, relax and allow your purpose to surface today. Then share it with others and make it happen. Here's To You!

Ann M. Preston

Finding Life's Passion

I was Meant to Share a Message
Elena Zanfei

"Dear God please let me die." That was the daily prayer of a lonely, scared, angry, young women. I was living in a personal hell. Alone with my pain, I saw no other way out. My life was producing a closed, insecure, lonely, needy, fearful, and negative person who hid behind the facade of a jokester. I was truly living the song, "Tears of a Clown." Surrounded by family rage and fear for my safety, my days were long and scary. My experiences were contaminating my beliefs and held me in daily pain, constant fear, and personal hopelessness. I was uneasy and uncomfortable in my own skin. So each day, in my sorrow and loneliness, I prayed for an end. Yet, deep inside was a vision; a longing to be happy, secure, confident, outgoing, open, and carefree. I wanted to connect with people and have a life of value.

The years passed and the prayer continued, until one day a thought arose. "Maybe God's not answering my prayer for a reason. What if I am not meant to avoid this pain but rather to overcome it? What if I could actually learn not only to survive my life but to make it a fabulous one? Could that be?" And so, my prayer changed to one for help. "Dear God, if you won't take these burdens from me, then send me the people, the information, and the insights to help overcome my life's challenges." On that day, it seemed as though God heard my prayer and soon after, the teachings began to appear. I found seminars, tapes, books, and people, all designed to pull me up, give me hope, and teach me what was truly possible.

It seemed as though I climbed out on the ledge of a 200-story building that day when I took my first step toward a new life. Never before had I gone to a seminar on my own or driven myself anywhere, not to mention into the "big city." I remember my knees knocking in fear as I stood in line in the hallway waiting for the seminar to begin. My heart was racing, and I thought I would die of fear. And in a way, I did die. The person that I was began to change during that weekend as I learned and explored new possibilities for the first time. I was 26-years-old.

I began to see how fundamentally alike all human beings are. I saw that I was not alone in my pain and shame and that there were hurting people all around me. I began to understand intrinsic worth, the true meaning of love, what integrity is, what it meant to tell the truth, the power of words, universal laws, and the meaning and gift of forgiveness. I began to understand how experiences shape beliefs, and beliefs govern lives. The epiphanies began, one after the other. "Aha" moments over and over. Wonderful seeds were being planted in the cold hard soil of my life that had once been overtaken by weeds and pests. I took up gardening–literally and figuratively. Over the 20 years that followed, dozens and dozens of seminars watered those seeds. Extensive books shed light on the seedlings. Thousands of hours of tapes nurtured the growth. Endless conversations plucked out the weeds that crept in. I began to water, feed, and fertilize those seeds often and well; enriching and fortifying them, encouraging a deep root system and a vigorous and healthy growth. Grow they did, and flourish they do. Gone are the distorted and damaging messages. The dramas, the apathy, and the loneliness of the past were being replaced with hope and strength and love. My light was being 'turned on' and I was drawing people to me as it began to shine brightly. I became what I had once envisioned.

As I sat at that very first seminar, even then I knew that someday I wanted to help others. This desire never left my soul as I climbed the corporate ladder. I was successful, excelling professionally and financially, but my soul yearned for significance. I was good at my job but was better at relationships. I understood people and therefore excelled in team work. I valued relationships, honesty, integrity and passion. I would always look for the good, and the beauty in people. Those skills were a far cry from what was needed for the technology projects I was managing. How was I going to be able to take everything that I had learned and teach it to others? This question would follow me for years. But God heard and felt my emptiness in the corporate boardrooms and understood the longing of my heart. He finally presented a Director who was wise enough to see what my life's true calling was to be. She suggested I become a coach.

What a wise women she is and what an angel she's become! Her words and belief in me guided me to the next step, out of the corporate world and into the world of feelings, support, encouragement, and relationships. Now, I honor all that is me by giving all that is me. I understand fear, pain, frustration, insecurity, guilt, and shame. I know what lies beneath–the potential that is there. I support my clients in removing the barriers that block their natural essence and help them realize their possibilities. I allow the creative part of me and my love for the home to be expressed through my interior design work. I use my passion and vision to reveal the potential of a home and to create beautiful spaces that house beautiful souls. I see the beauty now, in people and in their homes. I am well equipped and rightly skilled to help reveal the very best that lies beneath. After all, that has been my own journey. I woke up one day, not long ago, and realized that I am living the life I love–a life of relationships, a life of value; a life to live with passion for today, and hope for tomorrow.

Elena Zanfei

Transform Your Fear Into Focus!
Waldo Waldman

Fear is the greatest deterrent to success. It drains our ambition and denies us power to overcome challenges we face personally and professionally. When we let fear control us, we are destined to fail. When we control our fear and channel that energy in productive ways, we succeed.

How do you handle fear? Does fear control you, or do you control your fear? Do you become overwhelmed and give up, or do you face it with courage?

As a combat decorated fighter pilot, with 65 missions in hostile territory, I had to face my fears every day; getting shot down, letting down my country and my wingmen, and failing to accurately perform my mission responsibilities. If I wasn't able to handle this fear, I would have surely failed. I had to realize that I had the power to overcome fear.

The key to my success was in my ability to direct my focus towards three distinct areas. Obviously, we are not all fighter pilots flying combat missions; however, the same lessons of focus can be applied to everyday life. Here's how you can apply these fundamental principles for overcoming fear:

Focus on your mission – Accept responsibility for accomplishing your mission objectives and feel confident in your training and preparation. Why are you needed, and who is depending on you to get the job done? When you take the focus off yourself and your fear, and direct it toward how your mission will positively impact the lives of others, you find purpose in life.

Focus on your wingmen – Who is on your team that you can trust to get the job done? Who are the trusted and reliable partners in your life? Who can you turn to for love, inspiration, advice and courage? Perhaps it is your spouse, best friend, business partner, or co-worker. By focusing on all the wonderful, supporting relationships you have, you become more courageous and confident to tackle life's challenges. You don't have to fly through life solo, if you have faith and trust your wingmen!

Focus on winning – See the success you want in your imagination first. Remember, the body achieves what the mind has rehearsed. If your mind thinks failure, you are setting yourself up for failure. But if you train your thoughts to envision winning, if you imagine with perfect clarity overcoming your challenges with courage and achieving victory, then you are destined to win.

Finally, the most important part in handling fear is to embrace it. Accept your fear and learn from it. Don't fight it or attempt to eliminate it, as it is a battle that can never be won. By experiencing fear, we become more human. Fear teaches us that we are not perfect nor are we superior to anyone else. It makes us more compassionate as we realize the frailty of life and emphasizes what truly is important in our lives.

Regardless of where you are, when you transform your fear into focus–on your mission, your wingmen, and on winning–you are sure to be victorious in all that you do.

Now, Focus your Energy, Accept Responsibility^{SM}; and make it happen!

Waldo Waldman

Never Let Your Dream Die
Robert Rumble

Back in high school I was very shy and introverted. I truly wanted to move to Alaska and become a hermit. I achieved that goal 15 years later, with the help of my wife, who was on active duty in the military. During those 15 years my dream had gotten cloudy but I never forgot it.

By the time I arrived there, I had forgotten why it was important to me to go to Alaska. They say that people who move to Alaska are running either from or to something. Was I running from myself or was I running to the wide-open spaces to live in the backcountry away from the rest of the world? I felt like a salmon swimming upstream and I needed to find why Alaska had been my dream for so long. During this time of self-discovery my wife and I separated and eventually divorced.

For many years I tried to find my niche. I went back to school, managed several restaurants, owned several businesses, and became involved with several network marketing companies. The people that I met in network marketing were the most positive people that I had ever known, besides my mom. They not only had dreams and goals, but they actively pursued them. That was something that had been missing in my life. I started remembering my own dreams and why I had wanted to move to Alaska. I realized that being a hermit was no longer a dream of mine. I listened to tapes, read books, and sought out positive, motivated people. With the help and guidance of some of those people, my attitude started to change. Instead of seeing the glass as half empty, I started seeing it as half full, and eventually I saw it as half of what is and half of what can be. Two of the most influential people in my life during that time were Roy Minster and Mickey Sleeper. I no longer wanted to be a hermit, but instead wanted to travel and see the state. I felt like the fog that I was in had been burned away by the sun and I found my passion: traveling and being outdoors.

I landed several jobs where I was able to travel all over the state. One was for a company that traveled the state taking inventory. Some of the places they sent me to were villages that were accessible only by air or water. I was able both to travel and, if I planned it right, go hiking. I would find out about hiking trails in the area and would hike after work until time to leave.

FINDING LIFE'S PASSION

I decided to go back to school and finish requirements for my degrees. When I finished I was able to find work with two start-up Internet companies. One of my jobs was to travel Alaska, taking pictures and putting together virtual tours.

I started hiking more and more, first on the major trails close to Anchorage, and eventually moved further into the backcountry. I traveled by car, plane, and boat to get to my hiking spots all over the state. On the trails I would find stillness and a way to center myself while admiring the beauty of the wilderness. I would often reflect on my week and what I did right and what I needed to change. On the trail my mind would calm and I could be at peace with myself.

While on one of my long hiking trips, I remembered that I had once told my mom that I wanted to be a hiking guide. With some encouragement from friends, I started a hiking business called Anchorage Backyard Adventures. People would pay me to take them on day hikes. I found that I had to learn a lot more about Alaska than I had initially planed.

I learned that the Chilkoot Trail was a popular hiking trail, so I decided that I would hike it before I left Alaska. I knew that chapter of my life was coming to a close and it would soon be time for me to take my passions elsewhere. To hike the Chilkoot trail you need a reservation because only a limited number are allowed to hike each day. I made my reservation 6 months in advance. This was one of my more interesting backpacking trips, 4 days and 33 miles of history.

All along the trail there is evidence of the miners of the 1889 gold rush. Thousands of miners traveled over 1600 miles to Dawson City including the 33 miles of the Chilkoot Trail. Those 33 miles were, for some, the most costly. Many gave up everything to chase their dreams.

I still remember the day I crossed the summit. It was July 30 2000, about 11 o'clock in the morning. It was cloudy, wet, and chilly with a slight breeze. My only regret is that I did not allow more time for that particular hike, but I am proud to tell about it.

I left Alaska the third week of March, 2001, exactly 10 years since my arrival there. It was time to pursue new dreams. Now I follow my passion of traveling and sharing about my dream life in Alaska. While doing so, I also encourage others to keep their dreams alive and to go after them with vigor and passion. My passion for the outdoors has never waned; I still hike alone and enjoy the peacefulness of the outdoors. Although I have not overcome my shyness, I have learned to accept that about myself and have found ways to compensate, which makes me a better person. Who would have thought that I would go to Alaska to be a hermit and return as a motivational speaker?

Robert Rumble

THE FACES OF POVERTY: HOW TO REDUCE THEM
SYSTEMATICALLY
John Soulliere

Wow, what pain! I had constant headaches that were so painful the strongest anti-inflammatory and pain medications would not alleviate the volcanic pain in my neck. It was as if my head was constantly going to erupt. An associate recommended certain herbs to my wife Susan and me in 1993. The herbs helped, but only made the daily pain tolerable. Ironic isn't it? Modern medicine could not help in the way natural herbs did.

The headaches and neck pain came as a result of a neck injury that occurred on a Canadian Forces Base in Germany where I was a soldier and cook. At the time, I was training for a peace-keeping mission for the Bosnian upheaval. I was put in daily physiotherapy for my injury for five years, then released from the Canadian Military; they could do no more for me. My military career was ruined after 17 years of service, and I was given only a small pension that would not even support my family. Now, money was a concern and the bills were still coming in the mail. So my wife, being the person she is, went out and began what is now a successful career as an expeditor while I stayed home with our two young children.

Things happen for a reason.

I was not going to sit around moping about my injury. I wanted to find a way to help others in my predicament and further support my family. There was no way I was going into the corporate world; that would have been too physically demanding. I needed to be able to take time off when necessary because of what I call "extreme pain days from hell." Do you think the corporate world would have tolerated that?

After some research, I decided to become self-employed as an Insurance Broker/Financial Planner. Yes, I'm one of those guys and proud of it. The primary reason was to show others the importance of having disability, health insurance and life insurance, before getting sick or injured, and to have savings to fall back on that will take them all the way into retirement. You see, from my experiences as an Insurance Broker/Financial Planner, people don't ever imagine themselves becoming injured or unlucky. They don't think of something throwing their lives into an upheaval like mine. It always happens to someone else; not to them. Like hell! I'm lucky to still be here to tell them. It will happen to you at some point in life, whether through injury, sickness, or lack of planning.

The question is not if it will happen, but when.

This is how, in 1997, I got started in the process of reducing poverty, purely by accident.

Are you aware that poverty has many faces other than those you are used to seeing on television? We only see the child that needs clothes, food and an education. Yes, it's very important to feed and clothe them, but that is only one part of poverty. I hate to use the word poverty, but it's the truth: my family and I were there, and it was scary.

You see, poverty has faces in every country around the world, and that is sad. The poverty of single family parents. The poverty invoked by injury; the poverty invoked by illness; the poverty of retirement. These are good people with very little opportunity to break the cycle. And, even when given the chance, they don't know how.

Why? Because it isn't taught. It should have been a basic essential of graduating from high school, especially in learning the life skill of becoming a professional—not an amateur—in the art of talking to people. Everything we know about using the phone or talking to people in business is totally wrong.

I do not mean learning to become a sales person. We are all born as sales persons of the worst kind—like when we hammered our parents until we got our way as kids.

Selling is not the skill you need to be taught. We need the skills that Success University and Dani Johnson teach. Those basic skills are the power to do anything, anywhere. Another example is a DVD from www.thesecret.tv titled "The Secret." It is powerful, as you'll see. It really is "The Secret" to achieving anything.

Since most people use the internet, you will need to use it as well and learn to be self-reliant. Learn how to market any product or service by expanding on what you should have been taught in high school.

First, go and learn those skills. You will even learn how to talk your significant other into anything. These skills are the fundamentals—yes, the basics—to succeeding in any type of livelihood you wish to create. Without them, you will always be impoverished, and most of you will not succeed. It doesn't matter who you are: the injured, the sick, lawyers, doctors, construction workers, the average person. You must be able to:

1. **Think It.**
2. **Learn It.**
3. **Do It.**

The alternative is relying on your government's promise to support you.

We can be given a loaf of bread and be fed for a day, or be taught how to make and break bread for ourselves.

That has been my ever-growing passion in showing people how to reduce poverty systematically. I ask you to do the same. Again, it's as simple as: Think it; learn it; do it.

God Bless and Keep the Faith,

John C. Soulliere

Graduating From Personal Growth
Ron Wypkema

In the spring of 2002, my life changed forever. I had a profound shift in consciousness.

I should have been free from stress and anxiety. After all, in 1980, I began intensive personal growth through meditation and spiritual exploration. Then, in 1984, I started a private practice coaching people on how to live in the moment by getting free of psychological and emotional issues. By 1987, I was leading workshops internationally.

Still, I was puzzled, why after decades of personal growth, I was still working on myself. Despite knowing and teaching that now is all there is, I was still identifying with the mind and emotions.

On that day in 2002, it occurred to me that there must be a better way to get free of the problems of the self. I put aside all of my learning and emptied my mind. Suddenly, I had a flash of insight about how to dis-identify from memories and the emotions associated with them.

I immediately applied this insight to a memory that had been troubling me. Instantly, all of the negative emotions about that memory effortlessly vanished. There was a profound shift in consciousness. One moment, I was myself dealing with an emotional issue; the next, the self I had identified with my whole life disappeared like a puff of smoke in the morning breeze. There was pure awareness, oneness with all that is.

All of the problems, worries and concerns of the mind had vanished. Instead of the noisy mind, there was utter silence, serenity and joy. The now was so full; all ideas of past and future had dissolved. This eternal timelessness was freedom itself.

At some point, the mind came back. I chose another emotionally charged memory to work with. This memory was the last time I had seen my 86 year old father alive. I applied this new awareness technique to this second memory. Again the emotions dissolved into the pure peacefulness of the moment.

FINDING LIFE'S PASSION

As a result of being able to easily access this state of universal clarity, a complete system of awareness methods for freedom from the self and it's problems have come to me. Since it has come from the now and opens people to the now (the state of oneness), I call the work The Now ProcessTM.

I share the methods of The Now Process™ with people around the world. I teach people how to graduate from being a seeker on the path of personal growth. My life work is about Turning Seekers into Finders.™ Many tell me that in a brief phone session, they have received more transformation than they had in years of working on certain issues.

For over 20 years, I had been devoted to personal growth. The astonishing insight that came to me that day in 2002 helped me to recognize that personal growth work is working on symptoms not the problem! Amazingly, I did not have to fix myself, improve myself or get rid of any of the remaining negative emotions I had, in order for this profound liberation of oneness to occur. All the personal growth work I had done was based on a false premise, there is a separate self. Now it was clear why I was still stuck in the mind, dealing with "issues." Personal growth itself could not lead to freedom. Why? Because, despite having the best of intentions when we do personal growth, it perpetuates the myth of separation. It perpetuates the illusion of a separate self.

Regardless of whether a person is a beginner at personal growth, or has been on the path for 20 or more years, it is possible to become free right now.

The true being is freedom, peacefulness, oneness, wholeness and completeness.

The true being is love itself, eternal, pure awareness and universal intelligence.

Waking up to this universal oneness is possible in this moment. You don't need to improve yourself for years before it is possible to wake up to this reality. No time is required, since it is already here.

Until we wake up, the joke's on us, and no other joke has so much potential for creating so much suffering. The ego self is fiction. The "I" is the only real problem.

It is such a blessing to be of service in helping people to wake up to the light of the true being. As our identification with the mind and ego diminish, the limitless expressions of true freedom and higher potential are easily discovered. This moment is the moment to retire from seeking. This moment is the moment to wake up to find your true birth right.

Ron Wypkema

FINDING LIFE'S PASSION

YOU GOTTA WANTTA
Lee Beard

I remember it well; I can see it today as vividly as the day it happened.

It was during a presentation from a small-town basketball coach. He told a story about one of his championship players. It is a story of desire, and the miraculous changes that desire can make in our lives.

When he first saw her, three ideas were trying to balance themselves in his mind. First, he saw the potential for her to be a star, although less experienced coaches might have missed the tell-tale signs of future brilliance. Second, he noticed that she was overweight and out-of-shape; she had no business in sports–especially a sport that required constant movement and endless exertion. Third, he reminded himself that his was a small school in a small town, and the choices were few.

The story of chance is amazing. What if he had continued to look for some "perfect" player? What if he had decided that it would take too much work to convert this potential player into the real thing?

But the most powerful thing that I remember from his story was the result of his constant instruction; the interaction of the coach (teacher) and the player (student). When she found it difficult to run the simplest of drills, he told her, "You gotta wantta get from one end of the court to the other." It was the same at every practice: "You gotta wantta, you gotta wantta, you gotta wantta." It soon became her battle cry as she practiced and then, as she played: "You Gotta Wantta!"

The kid who wouldn't have been picked to play, became a champion.

This had such an impact on me that I made a sign which reads (you guessed it), "You gotta wantta," and placed it on my desk. Even now, it seems to say it all: "You gotta wantta."

For some reason, it sums up the essence of passion. A little dab will do, but a whole lot more won't hurt you, either. Can you tell that I've become attached to that phrase?

FINDING LIFE'S PASSION

As I go through the day, I often recall the words and the story. It brings a smile to my heart and a renewed determination to my spirit. I am reminded that "I gotta wantta" complete the task–no matter how tedious or commonplace or difficult–to get to the end of the project. Without that spirit of "gotta wantta," every obstacle is insurmountable; every challenge is a defeat.

I would wish for you the discovery of a passion that stirs your spirit and energizes your life so that each day is fun and each task is exciting. I believe that would make life better, and would make you a better person in the eyes of each one you meet. I hope to stir up your "wantta" so that you've "gotta" do it.

Lee Beard

AUTHOR INDEX

    Paula Adelman was born in Riverdale, New York and is a single mother of two highly motivated talented, successful young men. She is an LPGA golf teaching professional and started the first golf learning center in Israel. She accomplished this after taking up golf at age 40! Her motto has always been if you want something badly enough GO FOR IT. Paula's teaching philosophy is to teach an individual not a method.

Address: 100 Arlington Pl. #19
Edwards, CO 81632
Phone: 970-331-1134
E-mail: Golfmatches@aol.com

    Miss International 1996
    Vice-President, The MillionaireMaker Enterprise
    Vice-President, The Rainbow Portugal Organization

Websites: www.fernanda1.com
www.the-millionairemaker.com
www.rainbow-portugal.com
www.travelclub.com.pt
www.hakunamatatadesigns.com

    Family physician and real estate investor.

Address: 38 Sparks Close
Bromley
Kent, BR29GE
United Kingdom
Phone: +44 7879611592
E-mail: aderemibanjoko@yahoo.co.uk
Websites: www.aderemibanjoko.com
www.solaceministriesuk.com

    Lee is a former television producer and business developer. He lives in Arkansas when not traveling as the co-creator of the *Wake Up... Live the Life You Love* book series. Lee is an author featured in more than a dozen motivational and inspirational volumes. He concentrates on bringing the power of the *Wake Up* network to bear on the challenges of business development. You may contact Lee at: lee@wakeuplive.com

FINDING LIFE'S PASSION

Fabienne Fredrickson is founder of "The Client Attraction System™", the most complete Client Attraction training and coaching program for small business owners. Using her unique marketing principles, she went from a mediocre practice not generating enough income to having two separate businesses bursting at the seams, in less than 8 months each. Fabienne now teaches successful entrepreneurs how to become even more successful and profitable. For a FREE Client Attraction CD and information on her programs visit; www.ClientAttraction.com.

> Phone: 866-RAINMAKER
> Email: info@ClientAttraction.com
> Website: www.ClientAttraction.com

> E-mail: rina@marykay.com
> Website: www.mybeautyanalysis.com

A sought-after speaker, author and workshop leader, Bill Harris is Founder and Director of Centerpointe Research Institute and creator of Holosync® audio technology. Started in 1989 with borrowed recording equipment set up on his kitchen table, Centerpointe now has over 150,000 Holosync® users in 172 countries.

> Centerpointe Research Institute
> Address: 1700 NW 167th Place, Suite 220
> Beaverton, OR 97006
> Phone: 503-906-6001
> Website: www.centerpointe.com

> Address: Earth Star Publishing
> PO Box 1584
> Osborne Park, WA, 6916, Australia
> Phone: +08-9445-8133 Fax: +08-9445-8124
> Email: support@earthstar.com.au
> Web: www.meditate.com.au

BDS, MFGDP, DRDP, Licensed NLP master practitioner.
In his book, *Choose Your Reality,* Dr. Hudson teaches a new way of looking at life and the universe, a universe where our thoughts determine the very quality of the life we lead. Your mind helps create the reality around you.

> Websites: www.ChooseYourReality.com
> www.GDPResources.com

Known as "The Magic Mindesigner," Michelle is the co-founder of the Effortless Living Institute and is committed to making a difference! She is a professional speaker and inspired world traveler. Her mission is to assist individuals, companies, professional athletes and actors, to achieve their inner most potential. The top priority for her clients is RESULTS, through a feel good approach.

Address: Effortless Living Institute
3593 Granite Ct
Carlsbad, CA 92010
Phone: 760 720 1888 office
E-mail: Michelle@livingeffortless.com
Web-site: www.livingeffortless.com

A recognized Astrologer, Feng Shui Expert and Life Guide, Alice shares her passion with audiences around the world introducing a way to "Feng Shui the Self" through the ancient art of "Denjé." It was understood that aligning the environment of the soul is as important as aligning the physical things around us.

Phone: 808-598-2655
E-mail: alice@astrology-fengshui.com
Website: www.astrology-fengshui.com

Cameron is an author, speaker and stress fitness coach. He is a burnout survivor who has inspired 10s of 1000s to live it up without being washed-up. He has a Masters of Science in Public Health and has developed the "Cooling Down The Stress Soup Stress Management System." In his book, *Don't Eat The Soup As Hot As They Cook It!* he has distilled all the stress management essentials into eight powerful and very doable ways to cool off the stress soup.

Phone: 1-888-973-3388
E-mail: cameron@thestressfitnesscoach.com
Website: www.thestressfitnesscoach.com

David lives in Sooke, BC performing magic and running his company Magical Mind Enterprises Ltd.

Address: Sooke, British Columbia, Canada
E-mail: david@magicalmindonline.com

Pat is a successful business executive who started his own technology company in Dallas. More importantly, Pat is a Veteran with several Purple Hearts, a dedicated husband and father of four wonderful kids. He is also the author of *The Veteran Advantage*.

Owner, PJK Enterprises LLC
Address: 2405 Webster Dr.
Plano, TX. 75075
Phone: 972-985-0571
E-mail: pat.kiggins@veteranbusinessnews.com

Dan Klatt, the "Think and Grow Rich Guy," has served four years as the WealthSensei for people wanting to control the way they create their lives and master the issue of money–raising their net worth through increasing their self worth. He wants to "Spread The Wealth" by infecting you with the ProsperityVirus and giving you the "Think and Grow Rich Success Pack."

Address: P.O. Box 119
Sedona, AZ 86325
Websites: "ProsperityVirus: Get Infected": www.ProsperityVirus.com
Bonuses: www.Think-Wealthy.com/bonus-giveaway.html
Master "The Carnegie Formula" through the "Master-Key Class": www.MasterKeyClass.com

Dianea has been a practicing psychotherapist for 20 years, as well as the author of four books on the healing power of tears: *Tears Are Truth... Waiting to be Spoken*, endorsed by John Gray, author of *Men Are from Mars, Women Are from Venus*, *Everybody Cries* (a children's picture book), *Evolution of an Orgasm* (which integrates sexuality with spirituality) and *Everybody Laughs* (a children's picture book), recently published in 2006. She is a Marriage and Family Therapist, MA and RN.

Address: Ithaca, New York
Phone: 607-277-6440
E-mail: dianeako@yahoo.com
Website: www.makereallove.com

Jeremy is a life long Hoosier, residing in Indianapolis, Indiana except for four years in the U. S. Army. Having found his passion in canine search and rescue, he is a dog handler for Indiana Task Force One (INTF-1) and the Canine Urban Response Team (CURT). Jeremy is also the founder and President of The K9 Search and Rescue Foundation, Inc.

K9 Search and Foundation
Address: 5351 E. Thompson Rd. #127
Indianapolis, IN 46237
E-mail: www.jgleming.com
Website: www.k9sarf.org

Denise lives in Los Angeles and calls Europe her backyard. She spends time with family and large circle of friends where she finds herself recharged and committed to her work. Denise paints and does her clarity consulting along with her travels. She finds inspiration from dance and every life that touches her. If you are interested in a session with Denise;

Phone: 310-493-3071
Website with Denise's Art: www.Deniselynn.com
Website: www.ClarityConsulting.net

FINDING LIFE'S PASSION

Known worldwide as The "Naked" Vegan, Kimberly inspires people to take action through her radiant energy that embodies ultimate health and youth. As a health educator through radio, her rejuvenation retreat programs and information products and seminars–can take you from where you are now to where you want to be, and reach and sustain optimal health for youth and longevity.
> Naked Vegan, LLC
> Phone: 949-735-5883
> Website: www.thenakedvegan.com

W. Patrice Martin, a Life Skills Trainer in Baltimore, Maryland is fast becoming known as the premier deliverer of all knowledge related to "this thing called life." She is the author and creator of the S.H.I.F.T (Spiritual Healing in Feeling and Thought) System for Urban Revival©. Although this system will work for anyone who wants to change their lives for the better, Patrice's passion and compassion is for the physical, emotional, intellectual and spiritual revitalization of poor and working poor urban communities everywhere.
> Phone: 443-850-5932 and 410-682-2126
> E-mail: pm1527@comcast.net
> Website: www.spiritvisioncommunications.com

Scott McClure is an international motivational trainer and coach, that has been transforming people's lives through self discovery for the last five years. He has also launched a variety of successful businesses in entertainment and education. Before this, he managed multi-million dollar brands such as Nature's Resource and Friskies. He earned a BBA at University of Texas, MBA at University of North Carolina, and a variety of other certifications at cutting edge training centers throughout the US. He currently consults and shares outstanding investment opportunities. Please contact Scott if you have questions or comments, or would like more information about coaching, training, investment opportunities, or fund raising needs over $1 million.
> E-mail: wakeuplivescott@yahoo.com

Okneco received her graduate degree in Administration and Interpersonal Practice from the University of Michigan, Ann Arbor. Her extensive training and background in resolving conflicts, creating business strategies and innovative solutions while being value-driven has allowed her to focus on people's behavior and choices which led her to pursue leadership and business consulting. Ms. McTier is an executive coach, public speaker, and trainer who believes that people can excel and exceed their own expectations when their intrinsic worth, values and sense of purpose are aligned.
> Alphavision-Leadership and Business Consulting
> Phone: 1-800-791-2711
> E-mail: olmctier@yahoo.com
> Website: www.alphavision.org

FINDING LIFE'S PASSION

Tripp is a decorated veteran of the USMC. He holds a degree in Professional Aeronautics from Embry-Riddle University. Tripp is the CEO of EVI America, a global company dedicated to helping people around the world. He is also one of the top earners in the revolutionary home based business ITV VENTURES™. He is a success coach, public speaker and consultant to military members transitioning to civilian life through business ownership. He is married to Deja, has one son named Sebastian. He resides in San Diego, loves surfing and martial arts.

E-mail: Tripp_mehew@cox.net
Websites: www.ethosvisioninternational.com
www.itvventures.com/tripp

"The Internet Entrepreneur"
Designer, Internet Marketing Expert, Public Speaker and Author of "Home Business Success Kit"

Phone: 619-226-2877
Website: www.quickstartexpert.com

Matt is the founder and CEO of Success University, the #1 most popular online learning company in the world. As a dynamic speaker and young success story featured on television, Matt generates millions of dollars a year in sales while still in his 20's. His passion and biggest life's accomplishment is having helped thousands of people around the world achieve success.

Address: 13601 Preston Rd. #650 East
Dallas, TX 75240
Phone: 972-578-2100
E-mail: Matt@SuccessUniversity.com
Website: www.SuccessUniversity.com

Anita is founder and CEO of My Personal Best Coaching Group. A specialist in accelerated learning techniques and mental mastery, Anita works domestically and internationally with individuals, executives, schools, universities, sports teams, training organizations and corporate clients to produce excellence and translate human potential into peak performance.

Phone: +44-1256-332017
Website: www.powerfulmindtools.com

Susan will support you on your journey to empower yourself through her 30 years experience in facilitating: Personal Growth Courses; the Healing Arts; Reiki Master; Aromatherapy Classes; Distance Healing; Intuitive Readings; National Speaker and Workshops; Produced her own CD, Kuan Yin Loving Meditation; Connecting with Kuan Yin Workshop; Creates Inspiring Jewelry.

Address: Frisco, TX
Phone: 214-207-9277
E-mail: susanpaige@susanpaige.com
Website: www.susanpaige.com

Neil is President of Musical Motivator Productions. He is a successful speaker, corporate trainer and internationally known author of the book, *BE Success–Discover the Secret of Having the Life You Really Want.* Neil presents his breakthrough motivational programs, including BE Success for corporations, associations and non-profit organizations.

Phone: 972-418-1419
Email: neil@musicalmotivator.com
Websites: Free Success Tips: www.besuccesstips.com
Book info: www.besuccessbook.com

Professional Speaker, Author, Trainer
CEO & Founder of Freedom Builders
To learn how you can start Freedom Builders in your city, please contact Ann.

Address: Atlanta, Georgia
Phone: (770) 452-3324
E-mail: ann@freedombuildersinc.com
Website: www.FreedomBuildersInc.com

Ned and Cheryl Rae are Executive Directors and Founding Members of Success University. They have built teams numbering in the ten's of thousands and have served on several International Field Advisory Boards. Their gratitude goes out to Don Kennemer for his faith in them and Matt Morris for his direction and vision. In memory of Gerald & Juanita Hudson and William E Rae Sr.

E-mails: ned.rae@verizon.net & cheryl.rae@verizon.net
Website: www.pma.successuniversity.com

The #1 best-selling author, Gregory Scott Reid has become known for his energy and candor on the speakers' platform and his signature phrase "Always Good!" An experienced entrepreneur in his own right, he has become known as an effective leader, coach and "The Millionaire Mentor."

Phone: 877-303-3304
Website: www.AlwaysGood.com

The Anthony Robbins Foundation is a non-profit organization created to empower individuals and organizations to make a significant difference in the quality of life for people who are often forgotten—youth, homeless and hungry, prisoners, elderly and disabled. Our international coalition of caring volunteers provides the vision, the inspiration, the finest resources and the specific strategies needed to empower these important members of our society.

Phone: 800-554-0619 or 858-535-6295
E-mail: foundation@anthonyrobbinsfoundation.org
Website: www.anthonyrobbinsfoundation.org

FINDING LIFE'S PASSION

Author, speaker, and financial consultant and coach to millionaires world-wide. Jack Stafford Ross is an experienced entrepreneur who has become nationally known for his energy and integrity in producing high quality proven oil and gas projects in Texas, Oklahoma, and Louisiana. Mr. Ross also coaches senior executives and investors on health and spiritual matters.

> Phone: 214-364-2744
> E-mail: jackrossjr@yahoo.com

Robert lived in Alaska and still enjoys hiking and backpacking. He is an active member of Toastmasters, and a publish photographer. Robert does presentations; living a dream, communications, and goal achieving

> Phone: 530.541.4273
> E-mail: robert@psinvestments.biz

The Search Engine Scientist, author, speaker, internet marketer – specializing in traffic generation systems.

> Phone: 770-962-6384
> E-mail: sjslifep@mindspring.com
> Website: www.lifeplusvitamins.com

Matthias is the author and founder of: The MillionaireMaker Enterprise President, The Rainbow Portugal Organization

> Websites: www.the-millionairemaker.com
> www.rainbow-portugal.com
> www.travelclub.com.pt

Helen has a Master's degree in transpersonal psychology and, is a Jungian imagery therapist and author of *DANCING ON THE SUN; Imagination & Reality*. Ask for her free e-zine, *LIVING IMAGE* and look for *INNER COMPANY*, her forthcoming e-book on the image as instant transformer.

> Address: Bakersfield, California
> Phone: 661-873-7061
> E-mail: sugaron@cwo.com

Craig runs his own real-estate investment company, which buys houses for cash. His first book, regarding real-estate investment strategies, was released early 2005–showing families the power and financial rewards of uniting their resources to create dynasties. He is available to speak at real-estate seminars.

> Address: PO Box 472131
> Charlotte, NC 28247
> E-mail: craig@craigbuyhousescash.com

Matthew has been a Personal and Family Dynamics Consultant for the last 20 years. He is the founder and developer of the *Mastery of Loving Relationship Course* and travels throughout the country providing the course to those desiring a unique and complete understanding and practicality of how we can love ourselves and others more–and on purpose. He teaches individuals, couples, families and companies. Matthew is also in the process of training others to provide the program.

> Address: Minneapolis, Minnesota
> Phone: 612-721-2202
> Website: www.masteryofloving.com

"Why complain, when you can do something about it?" is what you will hear most from John Soulliere. He is known in his inner circle as someone who looks for the positive and reaches for solutions. He is a family man and an entrepreneur who is willing to go the extra mile in order to help his fellow man. His goal: "To reach for the unobtainable, while embracing what is within his reach."

> Phone: 1-403-238-8445
> Website: http://www.hbbseekers.com

Creator of *Wake Up ... Live the Life You Love.* With more than 12 million stories in print, his message is reaching an international audience. Steven E has joined many of his co-authors at seminars and lectures; they include: Wayne Dyer, Anthony Robbins, Deepak Chopra, Eddie Foy III, Donald Trump University, and many more inspirational souls. He and his Wake Up team are now developing a PBS show that will teach, inspire and touch even more people with his message: Reject fear and hopelessness in order to seize hope, purpose and meaning for a more fulfilling life.

> Website: www.wakeuplive.com

Emmett is certified with the National Guild of Hypnotist and an inspirational coach for Adolescents for Personal Achievement. He has a certification in Sports and Fitness Specialist, as well as a certification in Clinical & Complementary Medical Hypnotist.

> Public Speaker for Parents and Children
> Phone: 847-496-4828
> E-mail: sylvesterem@comcast.net
> Website: www.findyourhypnotist.com/sylvester

Finding Life's Passion

Brian is the most listened to audio author on personal and business success in the world today. His fast-moving talks and seminars on leadership, sales, managerial effectiveness and business strategy are loaded with powerful, proven ideas and strategies that people can immediately apply to get better results in every area.

Address: Brian Tracy International
462 Stevens Ave., Suite 202
Solana Beach, CA 92075
Phone: 858-481-2977
E-mail: mschiller@briantracy.com
Website: www.briantracy.com

Known as The Wingman, Waldo Waldman is an inspirational keynote speaker and corporate trainer on leadership and trust. A former combat decorated fighter pilot, Waldo applies his real world business and combat experience to building trusting relationships in life.

Phone: 1-866-WALDO-16 (925-3616)
Website: www.yourwingman.com
Email: Waldo@yourwingman.com

Dorothy Walker is the Vice-President of MetroPacific Bank, a SBA Loan Specialty "Expert," a #1 Best-Selling Co-Author, and the lecturer/writer of "messages from the other side." Dorothy helps her clients create their own multi-million dollar businesses by being a banking expert in financing small business, pre-qualifying loan applications for eligibility, expediting the funding process, and sharing their visions to accomplish short and long term goals.

Phone: 805-551-9858 and 818-395-0571
E-mail: metropacific@adelphia.net

Benson is a highly sought after clairvoyant Advisor/instructor, who (for the past 30 years) has been helping people from all walks of life to find their path to spiritual growth, happiness and success. He is the creator of the very popular and effective seven-step program called, "Feel Good Now! Discover The Hidden Messages Within You!"

San Francisco, CA
Phone: 415-752-0666
E-mail: feelgoodnow@comcast.net
Website: www.Feel-Good-Now.net

Artist of the Sea

Website: www.wyland.com

FINDING LIFE'S PASSION

Creator of Accelerated Spiritual Awakening, Author of Simply Being and The Audio Now Cards. Ron's simple, powerful system for Accelerated Spiritual Awakening is legendary. It offers a complete support system for people who are yearning for the peace, freedom and fulfillment that arise in evolving beyond the need for personal growth and self help. A gift to humanity, it offers direct access to higher consciousness and spiritual awakening. Ron offers worldwide teleclass trainings, live events, as well as Practitioner and Teacher Trainings in his acclaimed and revolutionary work.

Address: 311-1675 Martin Drive, White Rock
British Columbia, Canada V4A 6E2
Phone: 604-531-7674
Email: ron@spaciousnessofbeing.com
Website: www.spaciousnessofbeing.com

Elena is a cultivating coach who assists individuals in bringing out the best of themselves to the benefit of all their relationships. She specializes in working with successful people, professionals, managers, directors, entrepreneurs and anyone who directly or indirectly impacts the lives of others. Elena is a former IT manager with 20 years of corporate experience and 20 years of personal development. Elena has worked directly with executive staff to bridge the relational gap between management and staff by removing role based biases thereby allowing for a personal connection at all levels.

InVision Coaching
Phone: 708-782-4850
Website: www.elenazanfei.com

Learning Resource

Success University, the #1 most popular personal development website on the Internet, has been developed with one thing in mind: To teach you the *right kind* of knowledge that will raise the level of success in every area of your life.

We firmly believe that knowledge alone won't make you wealthy. We go to school for 12 to 20 years of our lives but are typically never taught the right kind of knowledge to be successful. In today's world, you need to THINK in a different way to achieve real and lasting success.

Success University now brings you *the most advanced online courses on SUCCESS ever assembled.* As a student, you will discover the secret attitudes, techniques, methods, and strategies that will skyrocket your success in virtually every area of your life. For less than a cup of coffee a day, you will gain access to the most advanced, cutting edge, online learning environment ever released on the Internet; teaching you how to be a success in your relationships, your finances, your health and physical well being, sales, marketing and much more.

You will learn from *over 50 of the most amazing minds on the planet* including Zig Ziglar, Jim Rohn, Brian Tracy, Les Brown, Cynthia Kersey, Denis Waitley and many more who collectively have helped millions of people achieve astounding levels of success. Many of the authors in this volume are associated with *Success University*, both as mentors and students.

www.successuniversity.com
Success University
13601 Preston Road
Suite 650, East Tower
Dallas, TX 75240
972-578-2100